SECOND WIFE

SECOND WIFE

*Stories and Wisdom from Women
Who Have Married Widowers*

Martha Denlinger Stahl

Good Books

Intercourse, PA 17534
800/762-7171
www.GoodBks.com

Acknowledgments

My special thanks go to my family for cooperating in the writing of our story. Rachel and John Daniel have both given me helpful editorial suggestions. I extend a hearty word of appreciation to all the persons who gave me their stories for this book. Next, I thank my Writers Arena for encouraging me to proceed with this project and for offering helpful critiques along the way. To Merle Good, publisher, thanks for catching the vision for the importance of this book. And to Phyllis Pellman Good, my heartfelt thanks for her skillful editing, and to Dawn Ranck for her artistic design of the book.

Cover photography by Jim L. Bowman, Bowman Images—Visual Imaginations. Used by permission.

All Bible verses, unless otherwise noted, are from the *Revised Standard Version of the Bible,* © 1952 (2nd edition, 1971) by the Division of Christian Education of the National Council of Churches of Christ in the United States of America. Used by permission. All rights reserved.

Design by Dawn J. Ranck

SECOND WIFE:
STORIES AND WISDOM FROM WOMEN WHO HAVE MARRIED WIDOWERS
Copyright © 2005 by Good Books, Intercourse, PA 17534
International Standard Book Number: 1-56148-483-0
Library of Congress Catalog Card Number: 2005010371

Library of Congress Cataloging-in-Publication Data

Stahl, Martha Denlinger, 1931-
 Second wife : stories and wisdom from women who have married widowers /
Martha Denlinger Stahl.
  p. cm.
 ISBN 1-56148-483-0 (pbk.)
 1. Remarriage--United States. 2. Wives--United States--Psychology. 3. Widowers--
United States. 4. Stepfamilies--United States. 5. Stahl, Martha Denlinger, 1931-
I. Title.
 HQ1019.U6S78 2005
 306.84--dc22   2005010371

With love, to
Omar, Rachel, and John Daniel,
who welcomed me into their family
as second wife/second mother
and encouraged me
in the writing of this book.

TABLE OF CONTENTS

AUTHOR'S PREFACE

It's like my writer friends agree: you write the book that you need yourself. I wish I could have read this book when I was considering marrying a widower. Not that it would have changed my plans to marry, but it would have helped me think through some of the questions on my mind.

While greeting family members at a viewing my husband and I attended, we met a couple whom we did not know. The man said, "My first wife was a daughter of the man who died." And when he said his name, I realized that his second wife, sitting there beside him, was one who had sent me her story in answer to my "Second Wife" questionnaire. I had never met her personally. These were two of the many wonderful people I learned to know in the process of writing this book.

I sent 60-some questionnaires and got responses from more than 40 persons. Some wrote their answers for me, and others told me their stories in personal interviews. It seemed that everyone I talked to knew of someone else who had a good second-wife story. It was difficult to know when I was finished with this book. There are so many second wives whom I didn't interview.

My own story is told with our real names, so I am being vulnerable and it's a little scary. My dear husband and two stepchildren have read and approved all my personal stories, for which I am grateful.

To protect the privacy of others, I have used fictitious names for everyone except my own family. The material I received came from women or men who married someone whose spouse had died. The experiences recorded here are from single women who married widowers, and widows who married widowers. Two of the stories are from the husbands' point of view, and one story comes from a single man who married a young widow with children.

Many women told me interesting stories about how God led them and their spouses together. Some were single until they married in mid- or later life, like I was; others were young when they married widowers; and some were widows who married widowers. Some had always hoped to marry, but others had decided never to marry and God had to speak quite loudly to convince them otherwise.

Many of the stories I heard did not fit neatly into my thematic chapters. So I've spread the stories throughout the book. Please note that, in most cases, they do not illustrate, nor relate directly, to the subjects of the chapters that immediately precede or follow them.

I've put distilled wisdom, gathered from those women and men I interviewed, into short lists at the ends of some chapters. I hope these are encouraging and helpful. Gathered here is earned wisdom.

1.
MY OWN STORY

Mmm, *what's this?* A lone letter addressed to me in beautiful handwriting. *Could it be from . . . ?* Quickly I slit the envelope and unfolded the letter. Almost holding my breath, I read:

Dear Martha, Earlier this evening I wrote a note to you asking you to be my guest at a lecture to be held at a nearby cultural center. But then I noticed that I have a church council meeting that evening. So I threw the note away.

I would enjoy getting better acquainted with you, and if you feel the same, perhaps we could correspond until, hopefully, I can avoid a schedule conflict. Let me know what you think. Thanks!

May our Risen Lord display His presence to and through you.

> Sincerely,
> Omar Stahl

Sitting alone at my desk on that March evening after school, I read and reread the letter. Here I was—single, 46, and busily involved as a public-school, second-grade teacher. I hadn't had a date for years and now this. My heart raced as

I tried to grasp the reality. Could it be that Omar Stahl wanted my friendship?

I can't say I had never thought about Omar. I met him at an information center where I worked part-time in the summers when I wasn't teaching school. Omar began working there during the April when his wife, Lois, was terminally ill. That spring and summer we worked together, and in September, the day before I went back to teaching, Lois passed away.

In December, Omar sat next to me at the staff dinner, and we chatted amiably. In March we talked briefly at our church conference's annual meeting. Omar commented on my lavender dress, saying, "You look like an Easter girl."

And now, later in March, this surprise letter—Omar Stahl asking for my friendship! I admit I was quite shaken up.

We wrote several rounds of letters before going out together. I enjoyed the letters, but I found it scary to think about where all this friendship might lead. Before we "went public," I told my mother and siblings about the letter and also told a few close friends.

Omar, an ordained minister and four years older than I, had been a missionary in Luxembourg and Germany with his wife, Lois. He lived with his daughter, Rachel, age 21, at the time we met, while his son, John Daniel, age 24, was away at college. He spoke German fluently and used stationery with German Scripture verses to write to me. In his third letter came another shock. He wrote, "Don't you see how I'm giving you free German lessons on my writing paper? Wouldn't you like to learn German? Would you consider living in Germany?"

So early in our friendship, the question seemed premature. Not understanding why he asked it of me now, I didn't feel ready to answer. I stewed over it until later when we discussed it in person. He didn't pressure me to give an answer; in fact, I brought it up.

About three weeks after the first letter we went out together on a beautiful April evening. As we walked toward his car, he asked, "Can you humble yourself to ride in a VW Beetle?" He knew I drove a blue, automatic, American Motors Matador, with four doors, air conditioning, and a white top. But as he held the door, I gladly slid down into the passenger seat of the little maroon Beetle. When he shifted the gears and we sped away, it seemed rather cozy to be close beside him in the Bug.

We had planned to go to a fine restaurant and then to a concert at a nearby college. Arriving at the restaurant, we found a long waiting line. He turned to me and asked, "What shall we do? Looks like we can't do both—enjoy a leisurely meal together *and* get to the concert on time."

"Well, I did want to go to the program." I searched his face to see what he wanted to do.

"Then let's go. Dinner isn't most important for me."

As we walked back to the car, I said, "But I'm not one to go without eating; let's stop and get a little something." So for my sake we stopped along the way at McDonald's, of all places.

"This is not my style for eating out," Omar said, "but what else can we do?" So, like American teenagers, we enjoyed a cheeseburger and milkshake at McDonald's on our first date.

A crowd, including many of our friends, was already seated in the auditorium when we arrived at the college. The usher led us to choice places near the front. As we walked down the aisle, I could imagine my friends catching their breath and whispering, "Look! Martha Denlinger is with a man! Who is he?"

And I loved every minute of it!

All this was happening during my 19th year of teaching at Paradise Elementary School. My good job, friends, family, and church kept single life from being boring. Yet I never lost the desire to be married someday. I had already concluded that if I ever did marry, it would probably be to a widower.

I enjoyed our times together over the next months. We did some pleasant things, such as visiting Longwood Gardens and the Garden of the Five Senses. One day I packed a picnic lunch and we drove to a campground. I thought the meatloaf sandwiches were quite a treat. Although Omar ate them joyfully, I learned later that he does not care for sandwiches. Another time we enjoyed preparing a meal at Omar's house, together with his daughter.

On one of our first dates we discussed the question about whether I would live in Germany. I expressed my opinion: "How can I answer a question like that when I don't know where our relationship will lead?"

But the question carried great importance for Omar. He reasoned, "I want to know that you are flexible enough to live in another country and that you are not tied to this particular place." He wanted to be able to leave the door open if he received an invitation to return to his beloved Germany. If I definitely never wanted to live there, he thought we should discontinue the courtship before we became too emotionally involved. That's why he asked the question so early. I tried to assure him that if I were faced with an invitation to live in Germany, as with any other big decision, I'd pray, and if the Lord gave me peace about it, I would be willing to go. He seemed satisfied with my answer, and our friendship continued.

In the days and weeks that followed, I struggled with a lot of questions. Many mornings I woke up early and thought and pondered. I even lost weight as questions whirled around in my mind. *Could I handle having grown stepchildren? Where would we live? I didn't relish the idea of moving to his house where Lois died. What about my teaching career? How would we handle money? Would I be able to keep my independence—with my own money to spend as I chose? And my cooking! My mother reigned in the kitchen, gladly making meals while I made lesson plans and corrected papers, so I was not a cook at all! What would we do with Omar's first wife's things? Would I feel that he really belonged to me?*

On a hot July evening of the day we attended Omar's niece's wedding, before getting out of the snug little Beetle, Omar surprised me by asking, "How would you like if we planned a wedding for ourselves?" I knew by then that I loved him but was shocked that he asked me so soon—not quite three months after our first date.

After hedging a bit, not knowing what to say, I finally came out with, "May I have a little more time before I give an answer?" He readily agreed to wait.

I continued to pray a lot. As we took a walk one evening, I asked him questions about subjects I didn't feel free to discuss before I knew we were seriously considering marriage—sex, money, and housing.

Then on that memorable evening five days later, after a pleasant visit and supper at the home of my aunt and uncle, the Lord gave me a wonderful peace about marrying Omar. Before he left that night I said to him, "Now I want to tell you that the answer to your questions is yes."

I'll never forget his hearty, "Praise the Lord." Before this we had been very proper and restrained, hardly touching each other, but now he started kissing me amid whispers of, "I love you."

On our engagement announcements we used this verse:

". . . I being in the way, the Lord led me . . ." (Genesis 24:27 KJV).

Then we began a great time of planning and decision-making. It wasn't all easy, but with the confidence that God was leading, we made it to the marriage altar on October 14, 1978. With affirmation from family and friends and with God's help, I began my new life, ready to face the many challenges ahead as a second wife.

AUDREY'S STORY

About six weeks after Jonathan's wife died, Audrey heard that Jonathan asked one of her relatives whether Audrey lived by herself. She began to think that he might call her. Just before Jonathan's wife died, a Scripture verse left a deep impression on Audrey:

"For I know the plans I have for you, declares the Lord, plans to prosper you and not to harm you, plans to give you hope and a future" (Jeremiah 29:11).

Audrey prayed that Jonathan would not ask her for a date until three months after his wife's death. On the very day after three months had passed, Jonathan called her, and Audrey agreed to let him come to see her. She hung up the phone and shook like a leaf—not that she was shocked that he called, but that God had answered her prayer in such a specific way. She prayed that God would calm her down for the evening, and he did.

As a single person Audrey had prayed, "God, if you want me to be married, prepare me for that person and prepare that person for me. And if not, help me to go on my merry way." The theme for their wedding was Ecclesiastes 3:11a, "He has made everything beautiful in his time."

REBECCA'S STORY

"For it is God who works in you to will and to act according to his good pleasures" (Philippians 2:13).

As a teenager, Rebecca viewed dating and marriage as serious steps and decided not to accept those responsibilities. Into her twenties, she kept refusing dates. Singing in a traveling chorus, a writing ministry, and caring for her parents kept her involved and enjoying life as a contented single.

As she neared retirement age, she was approached twice by widowers, but she refused them. Some time later the thought hit her quite forcibly: Can a single woman become too satisfied and too selfish to share her life? *About eight months later Rebecca had an extraordinary dream. "I was out somewhere in the dark when all of a sudden a big, bright light appeared before me. In the center of this oval-shaped light, a man's name appeared." She woke up and cried and asked, "Lord what does this mean?"*

The next day she didn't tell anyone at work about her dream. "The day was long and hard," she said, "because I was all torn up." That evening when she came home, she found a letter on the table. "I just knew who it was from," she said, "and I could hardly make myself open it." It was indeed from the man whose name she saw in her dream.

She waited about two weeks to answer, and then didn't give him a yes or no, but they kept in contact by let-

ter and phone. She lived in western Pennsylvania, and he lived in Georgia but was in Florida at the time with his mother.

Of her struggles that followed, she says, "I saw so many mountains—the seriousness and responsibility, his family (could they accept me?), leaving my comfortable place, breaking away from the chorus I had sung in since its beginning, leaving my many single girlfriends." Her nights dragged on with little sleep; her days seemed long and hard. When she entertained the thought that it would be easier to say no, her dream stood explicitly before her. "Within me I felt this is God's will," she said, "but I was afraid."

The Lord knew Rebecca needed confirmation that this was a step she should take, despite her earlier choice not to marry. One night at about 11 o'clock, she was so sick and worn out from struggling when she seemed to hear a voice say, You need to give up your will. She prayed, with tears, "Lord, if this [marriage] is your will for my life, I'll accept it."

"Then a burden rolled off me like I never experienced before," she said, "and a peace surged through me that I can't explain. I was a different person—free and happy." Rebecca had known the man and his first wife well, so they did not need a lot of time to get acquainted. They became engaged and soon married. "And now," she says, "we are happy together in the Lord."

2.
COURTSHIP—
PROBLEMS, FUN,
SECRETS

When we were dating, my family teased Omar about the fact that I couldn't cook. It was true; I didn't have much experience cooking. When I'd come home from school I'd mow the lawn, shop for groceries, or correct papers, while Mother was the queen of the kitchen and gladly prepared meals. My sister warned me that "The way to a man's heart is through his stomach." But Omar refuted this by saying, "The way to my heart is through my head." He didn't seem to be at all worried about my cooking. He said that whatever I prepared, if I could eat it he would eat it, too. However, after we were married I soon learned that Omar liked good food and had some definite likes and dislikes. I diligently studied recipes and soon learned to cook, serve meals to guests, and had my siblings raving about my cooking!

Another joke my family had was that a younger sibling may not marry before an older one. I had an older sister who was single. But nobody really took that seriously.

✳ ✳ ✳

Some women who got married after being single for many years ran into opposition from a parent or sibling. Kate's mother considered marriage an intruder, upsetting her plan for Kate to spend more time with her as she grew older and needed more help. Kate prayed about it and waited a while but decided to marry in spite of her mother's attitude. Her husband agreed that Kate's mother could live in the apartment in his house when she could no longer be alone. About four years after they were married, she came to live with them until she died about two years later. Kate did feel in the middle, trying to please her mother and her husband. But they survived it.

✳ ✳ ✳

Another single woman who lived with her parents got strong opposition from her mother. Even though they were ready for marriage, Evelyn and Frank put it off, hoping that Evelyn's mother would change her negative attitude. "I was an only child," Evelyn explains, "and was always close to my mother. She kept saying, 'Daddy and I are getting older and we need you, and now you're going to leave us.' She seemed to think I would go out of her life altogether. My friends were so happy for me, and several of her friends tried to get her to see that she should be happy for me instead of standing in the way." After they finally did marry, Evelyn's mother did a turn-around. Frank was so good to her, and she soon realized they weren't going to leave her high and dry.

✳ ✳ ✳

Rosene, who started dating Roger six months after her husband died, found her friends giving conflicting advice. "We received flack from nay-sayers—'What in the world are you doing?' —who thought it was too soon. And maybe it was," she says. "People meant well; they were just concerned, asking 'Are you sure you thought this through?' I don't think people on the outside can realize what an agonizing decision it is." And she wondered herself if she had taken enough time to grieve. "If Roger had not been through the same situation, it probably would not have worked. But since we both had similar experiences—seeing a spouse die of cancer—we were still able to grieve even after we were married."

As to timing, Rosene thinks marrying quickly is the only way she would have done it. She started dating before she and the children had time to adjust to being alone, before things settled into a routine. "Had the children and I been comfortable and making it without difficulty," she says, "I doubt I'd have ever done it."

Rosene's diary shows her struggle over the decision: "Lord, help me know what to do. Lord, I'm pleading with you. Make it clear to me; so clear that I don't have doubts. Please, oh Lord, speak to me." She says that even though God hadn't closed doors, she asked, "Is this really what I want to do?" Even then she didn't realize what a huge step it was.

Her concern was mostly for the children. "It was a big adjustment for them when Roger came along," she says. Despite the short time since their father had died, she had let them become almost too close to her, too dependent. She thinks that if she had waited two years to start dating, the children might have resisted and said, "No way!"

❊ ❊ ❊

On the lighter side, Reba, who started dating in her 40s, had some fun with the young women she worked with. When they talked about where they were going and what they were planning to do on dates, Reba would say, "Can I bring my date, too?"

They'd say, "Sure," and all laugh. They didn't know she really was dating.

A friend used to invite young dating couples to her home and serve them homemade ice cream. And Reba asked, "If I bring my boyfriend to your place, will you make us homemade ice cream?" She said, "I'll make you homemade ice cream if we have to go out and milk the cow!"

Reba says, "I was so tempted to take Abe there, but I just didn't quite have the nerve. We laughed a lot about that."

When they announced their engagement in the paper, the word spread quickly. The women she worked with had a shower for her, as did her sister, who invited her family and church friends. "It was a lot of fun," Reba says.

This older couple tried to keep their dating a secret for a while, and they had fun doing that. Abe used to drive out his farm lane with his lights off so the neighbors wouldn't know he was going out.

❊ ❊ ❊

Audrey gave Jonathan her garage-door opener. When he came, he drove right into her garage so her neighbors didn't see his car parked outside her house. At the wedding reception, he presented her with his garage-door opener!

❊ ❊ ❊

Pat and Edwin went to a neighboring county to eat at a restaurant where people would not know them. They had ordered their meal and sat there talking, when the waitress came over and said, "I see lots of married couples who come in and don't talk to each other; you look so happy together. Seeing you has made my day." They could hardly wait to get outside to enjoy laughter and talk about this. They weren't sure if they did right by not telling her they were a dating couple. She might have been disappointed.

Laura and Roy, too, kept their dating a secret for a while and had a little fun with it. She tells this story: "One Sunday a group from church went to a retreat center. I drove and took four other women. We listened to a program and then went to my home and ate lunch together. My friends left at 6:15 p.m. I rested, changed my dress, and was ready for Roy at seven o'clock. Later one of the women laughed when she found out how carefully I had planned everything so that they left before he came."

One couple sat together at her church, but tried to act as if it just happened that they were sitting beside each other.

A mutual friend served as a go-between for Eunice and Henry. Henry's wife had died in April, and in August Eunice agreed to a visit with him. They kept their first time together a secret. They went on a picnic and he brought all the provisions. That impressed her.

Some time before this, Eunice had attended a retreat where the speaker talked about why people remarry after the death of a spouse. Eunice asked, "Is loneliness a good reason?" She thought that it probably should not be the primary reason.

The speaker said, "It is often that, or persons might never remarry. It's okay if loneliness is the driving force. And we shouldn't be too hard on people for that."

Remembering this exchange helped Eunice to move forward with her own marriage plans.

✳ ✳ ✳

During the waiting and courtship, Scripture verses gave Reba divine reassurance, especially during times of uncertainty as to the outcome of the relationship.

These are the verses she had written in her Bible:

- "Commit your way to the Lord; trust in him and he will do this" (Psalm 37:5).
- "All of us who are mature should take such a view of things. And if on some point you think differently, that too God will make clear to you" (Philippians 3:15).
- "Whether you turn to the right or to the left, your ears will hear a voice behind you, saying, 'This is the way; walk in it'" (Isaiah 30:21).

- "The one who calls you is faithful and he will do it" (1 Thessalonians 5:24).

- "From the east I summon a bird of prey; from a far-off land, a man to fulfill my purpose. What I have said, that will I bring about; what I have planned, that will I do" (Isaiah 46:11).

- "Delight yourself in the Lord and he will give you the desires of your heart" (Psalm 37:4).

- "But those who hope in the Lord will renew their strength. They will soar on wings like eagles; they will run and not grow weary; they will walk and not be faint" (Isaiah 40:31).

✳ ✳ ✳

A widow who married a widower says, "I did more serious thinking [about this marriage] than when I was young and married the first time."

✳ ✳ ✳

For their first date, the man arrived at Elaine's door right on the dot at 7 p.m. This impressed her, since being on time was and still is very important to her. One of Elaine's favorite verses is:

"The Lord himself goes before you and will be with you; he will never leave you nor forsake you" (Deuteronomy 31:8).

✳ ✳ ✳

Ellen found healing for her first grief in her second marriage. She and her second husband got acquainted through mutual friends in whose home they had their first date. Ellen says, "The advice of a few close and trusted friends is helpful in getting started, especially in a second marriage."

SYLVIA'S STORY

Sylvia met Tony, an Episcopal minister, at their church conference center in Berkshire Hills, Massachusetts. Tony was then a 27-year-old husband and father, teaching courses to an eager group of teenagers. Sylvia was 15 years old, and, for the next eight summers, she and Tony both were part of two weeks of Christian community along with 80 other participants, many of whom kept in touch for years to come.

God sent a number of fine young men into Sylvia's life, but she felt, deep in her heart, that something was missing. So she chose to teach school, live with her widowed mother, and travel around the world whenever possible.

Tony's wife died many years later, and he wrote Sylvia from Falls Church, Virginia, asking her to marry him! She was then 53, and he 65! They soon married. She says, "I truly believe God's hand was evident in our meeting in 1943 and in bringing us together again in 1982— all part of his tapestry. God has been a big part of our life together these 18 years, and hopefully, we'll continue to be an example to others of God's love."

3.
PREMARITAL COUNSELING

When we asked my pastor to marry us, Omar also asked if he would give us counseling. Omar recalls that the pastor answered with a chuckle. He did give us a bit of admonition, but no scheduled sessions. Perhaps he thought that since Omar had been married before, and because I was 47 years old, we didn't need it. We made a good adjustment to married life, but premarital counseling might have helped make it even better. After a few years of marriage we attended Marriage Encounter and found it beneficial.

Pastors often excuse older couples from formal counseling because they think it is not necessary. Or they may feel inadequate to counsel people whom they consider older and wiser than themselves. It is often difficult for older couples to find a person who is sympathetic toward second marriages, and who is also willing and qualified to give them counsel.

Many of the women I interviewed for this book had no formal premarital counseling. Some who didn't have it wish they had and recommend it. Those who did have premarital counseling, for the most part, found it helpful and recommend it.

One of my friends who got married for the first time when in her 60s, and received regular sessions of marriage counseling, says that a third person can offer some objectivity.

✳ ✳ ✳

One woman found it a bit humorous. She said, "The young dean of my Cathedral, who was half the age of my husband-to-be, 'counseled' us one afternoon. He asked why we had chosen each other after all these years and what we would pray for as the years rolled on. It was very sweet and helped us articulate our unexpressed dreams for the future." She looks back on that afternoon with special feelings. She recommends this, because, "Maybe never again will a similar opportunity arise, to delve deeply into our hearts and souls, and into our dreams for the future."

✳ ✳ ✳

Another said, "The young pastor didn't know what to do with us. He planned for three sessions, but we had only two. It was okay, but not altogether necessary."

✳ ✳ ✳

But another had a negative response to it. "I had premarital counseling, and it made me mad. The minister questioned me like I was a 16-year-old kid, as if I didn't know what I was doing."

✳ ✳ ✳

A Christian doctor gave one couple questionnaires to complete and then compare with each other. This helped the couple to see how much they had in common and to be aware of things they might not have thought of.

The Myers-Briggs personality test is another good tool used in counseling. "We were amazed at how often we answered similarly," said one who used it. She also found the workbook, *Called Together,* helpful.

✳   ✳   ✳

One second wife said, "It was not in-depth. We didn't discuss specific issues like we should have. I don't feel I had a clear picture of what I was moving into. Maybe it's something you can't know until you get there. In a second marriage in which we each had a successful first marriage, we tend to forget that it takes time to make it successful. It is frustrating when you get into it and things aren't going as smoothly as in the first marriage."

✳   ✳   ✳

Outside of official premarital counseling, one second wife reported that her older brother shared from his marital experience, and she appreciated that. Another said that even though she was not married before, she had listened and watched how other married couples handled everyday problems. Another received advice from individuals, some who were apprehensive and others who were strongly affirming. One said she had received a good recommendation about her husband-to-be and knew him well enough that she trusted their marriage would go well.

Gathered Wisdom

1. Premarital counseling is helpful and recommended.
2. Counseling helps focus on issues you'll likely face later on, which you probably aren't thinking about when you're dating.
3. It is especially important for parents with children at home to have counseling, and to have the children involved in the counseling.
4. If partners are not through grieving over their former spouses, separate or combined counseling may be helpful.
5. Choose someone who has experience in counseling and, if possible, someone who is part of a second marriage.
6. Watch for signs of an abuser (See Chapter 15, beginning on page 150.)
7. Attend an Engagement Encounter before marriage (www.marriageencounter.org/moreee.htm), and/or Marriage Encounter after marriage (www.wwme.org).

AMANDA'S STORY

Amanda was in her 80s when her sister passed away, and she said, "I think my sister's husband, Jacob, will marry again; I hope he gets a good wife." At a family reunion that summer, none of Jacob's children were there, and Amanda invited him to eat with her and another sister and brother-in-law. He hadn't brought a place setting along and Amanda had extra, so he sat beside her at the table. "I didn't think anything about it," she says. "He was part of the family. But I later learned that he had gotten a different idea that day."

Jacob's sister lived near Amanda, and once a week he'd come to see his sister, and then he'd stop at Amanda's, too. As they sat and talked, she thought, he's lonely, and felt sorry for him. He kept coming, and one day he brought her a nice box of strawberries from his garden. She wanted to pay for them, but he said, "They're in appreciation for what you did for my wife." She thought, okay, it was nice to say that. And after awhile, she began to think, I wonder how long he's going to keep this up; I'm afraid people who see him come like this will get ideas. But she insists, "I didn't have ideas."

Then came the big surprise. One evening when they were sitting across the table from each other talking, he looked in her eyes and said, "I love you." That was the first she knew of his intentions. "If I'd have been his age or younger I may have gotten suspicious," she said. (She is six years older than he.) She reached over and took his hand; she thinks it was then that she said, "I'm just too old."

Jacob told her later that that kind of dampened things a bit, and he almost gave up. "But then," Amanda recalls, "one evening after supper together at my sister's, as we went out the walk, he says that I told him, 'We're not too old.' I do not remember saying that. But it gave Jacob new hope, and from then on things kept moving."

By September they were engaged, and they got married in January. By that time they both felt it was the Lord's will for them to be together. "I never knew anyone with whom I felt more free to talk. We like to be together."

4.
WEDDINGS

Omar and I had a hard time deciding whom to invite to our wedding. We opted to have the wedding at my home church with the reception in the church basement, where we were limited to about 220 guests. I'm sure more people wished to be invited, but we had to draw the line somewhere. We had Omar's children, Rachel and John Daniel, as attendants, and choral music by 40-plus nieces and nephews from the three families—Kraybill, (Omar's first wife's family,) Stahl, and Denlinger. John Daniel gave a welcome to the three families. We answered to the traditional wedding vows and added our own words of commitment to each other. It was a grand occasion, and we thrived on the many words of affirmation and blessing.

✳ ✳ ✳

Some people like surprises. Two college teachers kept their marriage plans a secret and shocked their friends by marrying at an unexpected time and place. Both were in Europe on separate assignments prior to attending a church conference in Holland, and they decided to have a European wedding. Still keeping the whole matter secret from family and friends, they had a civil wedding in Germany. Then, for the church wedding, they asked a well-known pastor to marry them at the conference location after one of the sessions. The surprise wedding took place in a little chapel with about 55 invited guests, who thought they were coming to a college alumni gathering. The bride said, "People received us in the right spirit."

✳ ✳ ✳

Another couple had a lawn wedding which they planned to have only family attend. But after the bride's nieces and nephews gave her a hard time, and her friendship circle threatened to eavesdrop along the road, the couple changed their plan and invited close friends and nieces and nephews to a beautiful lawn wedding. It was followed by a reception for over 200 guests.

✳ ✳ ✳

Neither Kate nor her husband wanted a big wedding, so they had their children and grandchildren and her mother to a small outdoor wedding. But they got some complaints from siblings whom they did not invite.

✳ ✳ ✳

Annette and Abner wanted all their close friends and relatives to enjoy their wedding with them, and they came up with a list of 400 guests. But the reception hall did not accommodate that many, so they whittled off 100 names—not an easy task. Annette wore an ivory dress; she was told white is for younger brides. She enjoyed every minute of the wedding, smiling so much that someone asked, "Why don't you stop smiling?" Her answer, "Because I'm happy." She says someone called theirs the "Wedding of the Year." Everybody seemed so glad for them.

She and Abner stood on a small rug for the ceremony. According to a Russian custom, the married couple keeps this rug, and when they have differences they can't easily resolve, they stand together on the rug and talk, pray, or laugh. Annette says they haven't needed to use it yet.

In the ceremony, before the vows, the pastor asked Abner's children and their spouses, "Do you give your blessing to this marriage of Dad and Annette?" They answered, "We do." After the vows, when the bridal couple knelt for prayer, his children and their spouses and Annette's siblings and their spouses, came forward and laid hands on them during the prayer.

Annette read two poems to Abner, one before the vows, part of which follows:

Dear God, I prayed all unafraid
. . .
"And let his face have character
a ruggedness of soul,
and let his whole life show, dear God,
a singleness of goal."
. . .
And when he comes, as he will come,
with quiet eyes aglow,
I'll understand that he's the one
I prayed for long ago.
      — Author unknown

Then after the vows, she read this one, entitled "Divine Guidance," which follows in part:

Often I prayed for someone—
Someone to really care;

Someone who loves my Savior
and believes in daily prayer.
Now I've found that someone
whose love is pure and true.
I know my prayers were answered
when God led me to you!
— Author unknown

At the reception, the song, "Welcome to the Family," sung by Abner's grandchildren, brought tears to Annette's eyes as her heart was touched by their loving acceptance.

✻ ✻ ✻

Lynn and LaMar, who also had many friends and relatives, decided to keep their wedding small. They invited about 100 family members and close friends to an unusual wedding at an historical museum set on beautiful grounds. Rain threatened the outdoor evening celebration, but, just before the wedding, the rain stopped, and a perfect rainbow arched over the building. Lynn's mother took this to be a sign from God and a blessing on the marriage, and she felt at peace. She had encouraged and affirmed Lynn all along, but struggled with the thought of losing her only daughter. Lynn believed the rainbow held a promise that God would receive glory at this wedding.

✻ ✻ ✻

During the meditation at Rosene and Roger's wedding, the pastor gave recognition to both their prior spouses. Among other things, he said, "No one will ever replace Ron. When he knew he would not get well, his prayer for you, Rosene, was that you would be happy. And Roger, no one will ever replace Lori, and the memory of Lori will live on. Now, God has brought Rosene into your life."

On their printed program appeared these words: "The flowers placed on the altar are in loving memory of Lori and Ron. They are so much a part of who we are, and their memories will live on in our hearts."

As they shared their vows with each other, Roger spoke his love for Rosene, and then named all four of Rosene's children and told them, "I am not only marrying Rosene today. I am marrying the family. I want us to be one family under God. I love you very dearly." Then he named his three children and told them he loved them. He said, "'As for me and my house, we will serve the Lord.' I want to be an example of a godly father." Rosene spoke her love for Roger, and then to all seven children: "I love you guys all very much and thank you for standing behind us in this wedding. I want our home to be a place where you all feel accepted. I want to be a good mom for you all, to guide you in the ways of the Lord."

All seven of the children had part in the wedding. (See Roger's story in Chapter 16, beginning on page 155.)

In contrast, Rose and Hans decided on a church wedding where the minister and his wife were the only people attending beside the bride and groom. Rose says, "My daughters adored their birth father so much, and I felt it would be difficult for them to watch me getting married again. However, they dearly love Hans, knew him and his first wife well, and have no regrets about our marriage."

Gathered Wisdom

1. The wedding is special, and, while you want everyone involved to be happy about it, you may not be able to please everyone. Each wedding is unique and will reflect the couple and their particular situation.
2. Talk it over, pray about it, treasure the event.
3. It may be a good idea to give recognition to previous spouses as part of the wedding ceremony.

REBA'S STORY

When Abe's wife was buried in September, Reba's parents wanted to go to the funeral. Reba wouldn't have gone herself, but she took her parents. When Abe walked in with his daughters on either side of him, Reba thought, He's a homely man. I don't think anybody would want to marry him. But soon after that, when she met him in town and he greeted her so pleasantly, she thought, I wonder if he is interested in me.

When she received the letter from a mission agency, asking her to come back to where she had served for many years as a cook in a school, she answered yes. But after writing the letter she didn't have peace, so she didn't send it and wrote another letter instead. "Talk about a step of faith," Reba remarks. "I said, 'I won't be coming back, and I can't say why.' I was sort of burned out and it was alright to have a change, but in my mind I thought maybe I would be getting married."

For a whole year she entertained that thought, while she and Abe had no verbal communication, no letters, nothing. She prayed that if marrying Abe was the Lord's will, if it would bring honor and glory to God, and if she could be a blessing to Abe, then she would be willing to do it.

She thought about his big house; she didn't want to live there. She was afraid he would raise tobacco on his *farm; she didn't want any part in that. But then at Wednesday night prayer meeting she heard him answer questions and gathered that he was deeply spiritual. At sewing circle, she overheard, "He's a flyer. He gets his work done, he does his cooking, he does everything." She never heard people say anything unkind about Abe.*

After one whole year, on New Year's Day, a cousin of Reba's invited Abe to a meal. Reba says, "That time I was a little bold. When my cousin told me they were having Abe for supper I said, 'Invite me, too.'" And they did.

After the visit, Abe did say he'd take her home, but he let her out at her house and didn't come in. He suggested they correspond. "That didn't please me at all," Reba remembers. But she agreed, and they wrote letters back and forth until spring.

Then they started going places together, and finally, after a couple of months, he proposed. They got married in September.

About the time of waiting, when Reba wasn't sure what was going to come out of it, she says, "I felt the presence of the Lord closer to me during that time than at any other time in my life. I think it was because I was talking to the Lord about it and not to anybody else. He was so real to me." (See page 19 for the Scriptures Reba wrote in her Bible.)

5.
WHERE SHALL WE LIVE?

For Omar, our American public auctions are theatrical performances, and he did not care to spend much time attending them. But I enjoyed them. By God's design, the house we decided we liked was listed to be sold at auction while Omar was out of town attending a conference. So I bid on the house, and the auctioneer knocked it off to me for a little less than the price Omar and I had agreed upon.

We decided to buy a house together which we'd call *our* house. I lived with my mother and sister, and he and his daughter lived in a rented house. Our "new" home needed to be located within easy driving distance to my school in a nearby town, to Omar's work east of the city, to the church where Omar pastored and to his daughter's workplace, both west of the city.

It seemed like a big order, in addition to being available at a price we could afford and pleasing to our explicit aesthetic tastes. According to Omar's daughter, Rachel, the house we bought had more character than the newer house we looked at. And it was located on the northeast edge of the city near the expressway with easy access for all three of us. God provided the perfect solution to my question about where we would live. We often thanked the Lord for our cozy home, and we lived there for 22 years (minus the four years we spent in Germany) until we moved to the retirement community.

A New Place for a New Marriage

Some of the women I interviewed preferred moving into a "new" house, rather than living where their husband and his first wife had lived or where the second wife had lived.

When Tony from Virginia married Sylvia from Massachusetts, he decided to retire from his church position in Virginia and come to Massachusetts to live and work in Episcopal churches in that area. They bought a large house together, intending for Sylvia's mother to live with them. However, Sylvia's mother died before they got married. They would not need such a large home for the two of them, but found it a great place to entertain Tony's children and grandchildren.

✳ ✳ ✳

Joyce lived by herself before she married, and her husband wanted to be close to the farm where he helped his son. They bought a house close to the farm, and she sold her house. Joyce likes living there but misses her friends and her church.

✳ ✳ ✳

Eileen, who married for the first time after she retired from teaching, owned her own home. Her husband sold his house in Florida and they bought a condominium there. Now they live in *their* condominium in Florida in the winter and in *her* house in central Pennsylvania in the summer. She is perfectly happy with the setup.

Jewel married a Canadian who owned a farm in Canada and a home in Florida. She moved out of her home (a three-unit apartment building in Pennsylvania which she owned) into a house which her husband bought in Pennsylvania. Then he bought a newer house in Canada for them, about a mile from his home farm. Jewel is thankful they can live in a place that is new for both of them. She had a little more difficulty moving into his home in Florida where he had lived with his first wife, especially since he was reluctant to make changes. But after 10 years, she says she has now made enough changes that "it is more like me."

Jewel decided to keep her apartment building in Pennsylvania, even though sometimes it is difficult to maintain it at a distance. Her husband is eight and a half years older than she is. If he should die before she does, and since they did not deed the houses in Canada or Florida in both of their names, she felt she needed the security of having a place to go back to.

Cheryl says, "Before we were married, we looked for a house we could call *our* home." But that didn't happen, so she moved into his place and was happy there. Later, her husband found a place for sale near his workplace, so they looked at it and bought it. Cheryl comments that they down-sized and now enjoy "our new home."

✳ ✳ ✳

At Home in the Husband's House

A number of my single friends who married widowers may have wished to have a new place they could call "our" home, but for various reasons found it logical to move into their husband's house.

✳ ✳ ✳

Audrey, who married for the first time after age 60, thought she owned the more desirable house, but her husband-to-be wanted to live closer to his work. They looked for a house they could buy together but didn't find a suitable one, so Audrey made up her mind to be happy in his house. After a time she realized that the move was the best decision. Audrey knew her husband's first wife and didn't mind at all living where she had lived.

✳ ✳ ✳

Amy had a home of her own, and her husband-to-be still lived and worked on his farm. After they married, they talked about buying a house together after she sold her house and he turned the farm over to his son. But that never happened, because a short time after they were married, he became ill and died. It worked well for Amy to be living on the farm at that time. She says being there contributed to her bonding with his family.

✳ ✳ ✳

Evelyn lived with her parents before her marriage. Her husband had moved off his farm to a small home only a couple of years before his first wife died. Evelyn says she didn't mind living in his house. She hadn't known his first wife.

* * *

One woman was happy to move into her husband's "elegant" house. Another said, "His home was more beautiful than any place I had ever lived."

* * *

Church and family were deciding factors for some. Julie, from Ohio, says before she even agreed to date her husband-to-be, he explained to her in a letter that he felt responsible to the church where he was a deacon, so she knew from the start she'd move to Pennsylvania if she married him.

* * *

Others wanted to make the adjustment easy for children who were still at home. One woman whose new husband had young children says she made as few changes as possible to the house, so that it would still seem like home to her husband and his children.

Married to a Farmer— No Choice But His Farm

Maria in Germany married young and did not own a home of her own. She came to her husband's house, his farm, and his children. She had difficulty feeling at home there.

* * *

Vera and Marcia, each single before marrying farmers with young children at home, found it logical to move into their husbands' houses. Both had lived with their parents and had grown up on farms, so cows and hard work were not new to either one of them.

✳ ✳ ✳"

Another second wife found the big farmhouse overwhelming at first, but she adjusted well.

✳ ✳ ✳

Even Elva, a city woman, moved to her husband's farm and loved it.

At Home in the Wife's House

Myrtle married for the first time at age 66. She had her own home, and her husband-to-be, who was from another state, suggested that he live with her. She was a career woman, and neither of them wanted her to stop her teaching and writing activities.

✳ ✳ ✳

Annette, single before marriage in her 50s, had several options—live at his house, live in one of his rental properties, or have him move into her house. Being 18 years older than Annette, Abner wanted her to be able to be near her family and friends where she'd feel surrounded after he was gone. She was willing to sell her place, but appreciated his consideration. He came to live at her home where they plan to live until they move to a retirement community.

Widows Who Married Widowers

Ellen was glad they did not choose to live in either her house, or her husband's house, where each had lived with their previous spouses. She had too many memories of her first husband tied to the house where she and he had lived together.

✼　✼　✼

Rose, who had been a widow for 12 years, also requested a fresh start. When Hans asked her if she would like to live in his house in suburban Philadelphia, she told him, no, she wanted a place where they'd make a fresh start together. He asked her where, and she said, "Anywhere in Lancaster." She had visited nearby Lancaster and loved it, and he had previously lived there. They bought a house and enjoyed living in Lancaster for six years, until they moved to an apartment at a retirement home.

✼　✼　✼

When Henry took Eunice to see his house, she was overwhelmed. "It was full of antiques—bottles and dishes, and so on. In a closed-off part of the house I noticed a musty smell that turned me off," she recalls.

After looking at his house on their first date, Henry asked her how she'd feel about moving into it. "I don't know," was her noncommittal answer.

On the way to the car she dropped a hint from a friend who had called that very morning. She told Henry, "I asked my friend if she had any counsel for me. And she said, 'Yes, I have learned a few things. I'd say start new—both the place where you live, *and* the church you attend.'"

A few days later Henry called and said, "I couldn't sleep last night. It wouldn't be at all fair to ask you to move in here." He had 18 acres and was still farming. He wanted to get rid of all his "stuff" and didn't know how.

Eventually, Henry decided to have a sale, and they started looking for a house together, even before they were engaged. Eunice asked, "But what if something happens that our relationship doesn't continue?"

He said, "Then I'll own the new house and I can rent it to you, or I'll figure out something else to do with the house."

He bought a place they both liked, and, soon after their engagement, Eunice moved into it just at the time when she needed to move out of the place where she was house-sitting. Two months later they were married, and now they enjoy living together in a "new"place for a new start, just as her friend had recommended.

* * *

As with the single women, many widows found themselves in circumstances that made it practical to move into their husbands' homes.

Susan had sold her home and household furniture and was living with her daughter when George came on the scene. George lived in and owned a well-furnished house. If she had still owned her own home, it might have been difficult to give it up. She says, "George made me feel like his home was mine. He told me, 'This house is now yours and everything in it. If you'd like to change anything, that's up to you.'"

* * *

Pat had planned to stay in her house as long as she lived, but when Edwin came into the picture, she thought, "Maybe I am ready to give up this big house." First she asked him how he'd feel about moving to her house. He wasn't eager for a place with so much work; it had a large lawn and garden. Then he asked if she'd feel okay about coming to his smaller house where he and Ernestine had lived in retirement. She liked it and thought she wouldn't mind. However, when she visited the house with Edwin, Pat "saw" Ernestine all through the house. She thought, "These are her things; I'm robbing her." But after working through it, and bringing a lot of her own things, Pat feels at home there.

* * *

For my friend Thelma, the housing solution seemed obvious from the beginning. She married a widower who had a nearly new house. Even though she owned a gorgeous, large home, she says, "Having known his first wife, I wasn't bothered at all about living in their house. Everything fell into place. We never discussed buying another house for us." Thelma likes the nice quiet neighborhood and, as she is getting older, appreciates having a smaller house to take care of. And her daughter was happy to take over Thelma's former home and business.

Janette remarried when her own children, and four of her new husband's, were still at home. They moved to his house, which seemed the thing to do because it was near his work and his church. His children didn't want things changed, although her husband said she could make changes. Janette did not know his first wife, but somehow felt her presence there with them. Janette says, "I kept telling myself, 'God led you here,' but I still didn't feel that it was my home." After nine years they moved to another property.

In a few cases the widow had the most appropriate house and her husband moved into hers.

Norma had a three-bedroom, fully furnished house in New York, and her husband lived in a small apartment in a retirement home in Canada. He suggested that he move to her house. There they had plenty of room for visits from both his and her children and grandchildren.

Beulah, a retired missionary living in her own home, married another missionary who had recently returned from overseas and did not have a house. He moved in with her.

Gathered Wisdom from Second Wives

1. It is helpful to live in new surroundings so that together you can make a fresh start.
2. Start on neutral turf, especially when bringing children together from two families.
3. Where there are children living at home, in either one family or in both, bring them into the discussion and let them help to decide where the "new" family should live.
4. While moving to a house new to both spouses seems ideal, it is not always practical. It is possible to adjust and be happy living in a house where one or the other had lived with a former spouse.

LAURA'S STORY

Laura was the bookkeeper at an organization to which Ray had loaned some money. It was Laura's duty to give him the check repaying the loan and to pick up the note. Early one morning in March, she received a call from Ray, saying that he could stop at her house that evening for the check and suggested that they eat together. To the contrary, she insisted she would stop at his home to pick up the note and deliver the check.

"His call was a great surprise to me," Laura says. "I refused his offer because I didn't want to be seen with him until I had time to consider what I would do about marriage. I had decided never to marry."

But Laura remembered a question she had heard discussed at a Sunday School convention: "What does the church do for the widower?" She asked herself, Am I being selfish if I want to live my life by myself?

Six months later, in June, Laura gave Ray a message, saying that if he still wanted to take her out for a meal she was willing, In July he called and asked to take her out for lunch. Their courtship developed in secret at first.

On October 21 he asked if she was willing to marry him. Later they sealed the engagement at his house with Scripture and prayer. They celebrated, first with his children, then at the end of October, on her birthday, at the place where she worked. There they divulged their secret by presenting a cake with their names and the word "engaged." They were married in December.

Laura says, "I told myself that the marriage would be my 'mission task' and, as God promised enabling for a mission calling, so he would enable me in the marriage and whatever was associated with it." Her verse is,

"But he said unto me, 'My grace is sufficient for you, for my power is made perfect in weakness'" (2 Corinthians 12:9a).

6.
FIRST WIFE'S THINGS AND PHOTOS FROM THE FIRST MARRIAGE

A beautiful lamp with a ceramic base sat on the piano in our newly established home. I looked at the inscription, "Omar and Lois," on the base, with mixed feelings. Omar's sister had crafted it and given it to them as a wedding gift. A set of serving trays also had their names on them. Omar's memories and aesthetic attachment kept him from giving up such things. But Omar's grown children didn't like having us display or use these items.

The lamp problem got solved inadvertently when the base cracked. My creative husband removed the broken base and attached a wooden one in its place, leaving the part with the ceramic birds as a beautiful reminder of his sister's handiwork. Now everyone involved felt good about seeing it in our living room.

Lois's souvenir spoon collection, mounted on a wooden maple-leaf holder made by a friend of ours, graced our dining room wall. I polished the spoons once in a while and enjoyed looking at them. We used lots of other things that Lois and Omar had—wedding gifts, souvenirs from Europe, and ordinary household items.

Omar said, "Some husbands would not give a hoot about items that are purely decorative, but I do." So my things and his (including hers) were all part of our collection of household items, and we liked sharing them together.

Recently our daughter Rachel reminded me of an incident I had forgotten about—probably because it was not as traumatic for me as it was for her and John Daniel. When Rachel and John Daniel visited Omar and me while we were living in Germany for several years, they discovered that I was using the pillowcases, made by their mother from colorful feed bags, as cleaning rags. They approached me cautiously with their stories about how as young children they hugged their pillows with these colorful cases and always took them along on their frequent moves from place to place. The pillows were a sort of security blanket for each of them. Of course, I had no idea that I was misusing such valuable treasures, and so I quickly rescued them. Fortunately, they turned out quite nicely after being laundered and ironed, and to this day John Daniel and Rachel each keep one of them tucked away in a special place where each can look at these special warm fuzzies from their childhoods.

Ways of Dealing with the First Wife's Things

As I talked with others, I found various ways women deal
with the first wife's belongings:

Pat says, "Our home has a blend of his/hers and mine/my
former husband's things, but now they are ours." I find that
to be a similar theme among the women I interviewed.

✳ ✳ ✳

My good friend Thelma, a widow who married a widower, told me, "I cleaned out the cupboards and moved my
things in, but the living room suite is his. Mine would not
match in here, and my daughter who has my house kept it
and was glad for it."

She pointed out a drop-leaf table in the dining room, "I
brought that along, plus the coffee table which my first husband gave me. This dining room suite is mine. I kept his cur-
tains; I like them." They let his children pick out what they
wanted; the children took some of the dishes, cookbooks,
quilting items, and so on. Then Thelma and Mark took lots
of boxes, of both his and her things, to an auction.

✳ ✳ ✳

As I walked into my friend Evelyn's kitchen, I saw her
strawberry motif on almost everything, so I knew what belonged to her. But in the living room I admired an afghan, and
she said, "That was his first wife's. The things in the big
hutch are all hers. It's hard for him to get rid of things. Some
day they will go to his children." Evelyn doesn't mind using
the first wife's household goods, but gradually more and
more things of her own choosing appear in the living room.
Things are a problem in another way for Evelyn; not his first
wife's, but *his* things. He's a hopeless pack rat and has the
garage, basement, and storage area bulging with flea-market

stuff. His pickup truck is running over. He and Eveyln both love buying, selling, and flea-marketing, but she can't see why he doesn't get rid of the accumulation that he isn't selling.

One woman, who married for the first time near age 50, moved into her husband's big farmhouse. Money from her parents, in like amount which they had given to her sisters who married earlier, enabled her to buy a new stove, refrigerator, and living room suite. She bought a new bedroom suite with her own money. Then her husband didn't think the bedroom carpet went with the new suite, so he bought new carpet. With wedding gifts—dishes, a cedar chest, and so on—she enjoyed having a lot of new things, while also using some of the first wife's goods.

Alma, another single who married a widower, says, "When we returned from our honeymoon, we found that his single daughter had moved all of her mother's good dishes out of the cupboards." Alma appreciated this. "I felt she did it for my sake," she says.

Joanne's husband suggested that they get new bedroom furniture. They also emptied the cupboards and gave their contents to his children. This allowed her much-appreciated space to store their wedding gifts.

Annette and Abner, who live in Annette's house, use both his and her things but keep them separate. She has a basement where they entertain, and his things are down there—furniture, dishes, silverware, tablecloths, and photo albums. Eventually he plans to give these things to his children.

* * *

Marie related a story which shows the feelings a child had for his mother's things. "There was an old Christmas cactus in the house which didn't bloom much and didn't look nice. One day I put it in the trash. Later I found our son in the basement, taking it out of the trash and re-potting it. It was something that had belonged to his mother. I felt bad about having thrown it away, never thinking what this plant might mean to him. He put it in his shop in the barn, and I'm not sure how long he kept it."

* * *

Some second wives were offered first pick of the first wife's things:

Rebecca's husband's children asked that she come to his home in Georgia and take anything she wished to have. She said, "I can't do that." She wanted him and the children to decide what was to be done with everything. Then, if anything was left that she could use, she wouldn't mind bringing it to their home. They did that, and then she went to Georgia to choose a few things. They offered the rest, mostly little things, to people at their church. Her husband brought the washer and dryer, his desk, and an easy chair. Their house is modestly furnished, and they are both happy using *their* things together.

* * *

Myrtle's husband and family also offered her first choice of his first wife's things. After she and the family chose what they wanted, he sold what he called his junk. He never returned to his earlier home to see it sold. Things he brought along to her house he willed to her.

Things Given to Children, Sometimes Divided in Creative Ways

Amanda told her husband that his first wife's things belonged to his children. When she assured him that she had things to replace them, he put the things on five piles—one for each child—and somehow they had a method of knowing which pile each should receive.

Before their marriage, Audrey's husband-to-be invited his children to choose what they wanted from his first wife's things without any money being exchanged. They all appeared to be satisfied. The things that were left, which Audrey didn't wish to keep, he sold at auction. Audrey brought most of her own furniture when she moved into her husband's house.

Jewel, a single woman who married a snowbird, says, "Fortunately, most of the personal things were taken out of the house in Florida. There did remain some pictures, afghans, quilts, and dishes." Later, Jewel gave an afghan to her stepson for his birthday and told him his mother had made it. To her husband's only daughter she gave two quilts her mother had made. Both children really appreciated receiving these. She has several more afghans and quilts which she will give to her other stepchildren. She has given a number of figurines from the house in Florida to grandchildren. More of the first wife's dishes and furniture will go to her children when Jewel and her husband no longer need them.

When Elaine married, her husband had children who continued to live with both of them. She remembers the evening the children divided some of their mother's things. "The children were with us in the living room. I sat at the end of the room on the steps. This was theirs to work through, and I didn't want to be in the way or intimidate them." But one of the daughters wanted to see Elaine's expressions and know how she was feeling as they made decisions about the items. "I appreciated her sensitivity," Elaine says.

* * *

Marie packed most of the china, glassware, and silverware away for the children, and then gave the things to them when they married or had homes of their own. But she still uses the first wife's cookware and a few of her dishes. She says, "Whatever was good enough for my good friend was good enough for me."

* * *

Rosene cut her first husband's shirts into patches. Her four children will each get a comforter and a pillow made of patches from their birth father's shirts.

About the Photos

In the first year of our marriage, I got a strange feeling whenever I looked at photos of Omar and Lois when they were younger—Omar, slim with lots of black wavy hair. I didn't know him then. But I decided I would try to think that the Omar in those pictures was Lois' husband. The Omar I know is my husband. As time went on, I enjoyed looking at the old pictures and learning about his earlier life.

Two women had a similar story. When they visited their husbands-to-be's home before marriage, each man had a photo of his first wife in the bedroom. They didn't feel comfortable with this, and in both cases the photos were no longer displayed after their marriages.

In most of the second wives' homes I did not see photos of the first wedding sitting around, but many kept them in drawers or in albums on the shelf. The albums are a source of joy for many, since numerous second wives did not know the first family when the children were little, and the pictures help them to get better acquainted.

Some do have pictures of the first wife and/or family on display. One says they have a family picture with her husband's first wife on it in the guest bedroom. Another has the family picture, taken shortly before the wife's death, in an upstairs bedroom which they seldom use. She says, "Our bedroom is downstairs, and I doubt if my husband even knows those pictures are there."

One second wife does have a family photo with the first wife in it displayed in the living room. "After all," she says, "she is a part of the family."

Another says, "I have no problems with first-marriage pictures, because they represent a vital and important part of the family's life." And another says, "She is still the children's mother and the grandchildren's first grandmother. They should keep a memory of her."

Many have pictures of children and grandchildren—both hers and his—displayed in the living room.

One wife says that her husband has his photos put away in boxes or albums. They will someday go to his children if they want them. She recently put her old photos in an album as a history for her children.

One says the six children had pictures of their mother in their rooms. Other photos were in albums.

"As for photos," another says, "When I moved to his house, there was a drawer of photos. I don't do well assembling photo albums or scrapbooks, so there the photos are, waiting to be sorted and divided. Many snowstorms have passed and still the photos wait, and the pile grows. My goal is to divide them among the six children."

Another felt all right about having the photo of her husband with his first wife displayed in the living room, but her husband put it in a drawer. She got it out and he put it away a second time, so she decided to let it stay in the drawer.

In one home you can see wedding photos of the second wife's first and second weddings, as well as a 50th-anniversary photo of her second husband and his first wife. Photos of both families are also displayed. She knew both her husbands' previous wives and feels good about having these photos exhibited.

Some have devised creative ways to preserve the photos. One chose to make composites of the family's eight children and arranged them on placemats to be used as wall hangings.

Another second wife explains, "I'm keeping an individual decorative box for each of the 14 grandchildren." Into each box will go pictures of their parents and grandparents in their early days, recent pictures of each child at family gatherings, programs of their first grandmother's funeral service, and so on. "I had written a story about five of the grandchildren's first visit two months after we were married, which appeared in a magazine. Copies of that issue will go into each box." She and her husband lost a seven-year-old grandson to cancer. Her husband wrote a poem and read it at his funeral. An uncle wrote something for the funeral. There were pictures taken at the funeral, with all the little ones kneeling down around and looking into the gravesite. These items will go into the boxes. Her husband started writing his memoirs several years ago. If he ever finishes, they will go in. She also clips stories from the local papers which she thinks might interest them later in life. "Sometimes," she said, "I feel overwhelmed by this project and wonder why I ever started! I have one main box where I put stuff and, as I have time, sort it into the 14 boxes. Perhaps I'll give them as wedding gifts or 25th-birthday gifts."

In one home, a photo of the first wife with her children in a mission-work setting is displayed. The second wife, who was a good friend of the first wife, said, "I wanted his children to know that memories of the past will always be a part of us." She also plans—some snowy day—to make a creative-memories album for each of the children, putting family pictures in the albums.

Pictures of previous spouses? One couple said, "Just not in the bedroom."

Gathered Wisdom

1. Remember that the first wife's things are also your husband's things. There is no need to do away with all of those things.

2. Try to find out what items have special significance for the children and preserve them carefully. They can be given to the children right away, stored to give to them in the future, or even used in the new home and given to the children later.

3. The displaying of family photos may be a sensitive issue in the early days of a second marriage. As time goes on and a bonding between all members of the "new" family takes place, the photos will likely become less of an issue. Each family will need to decide what to do with them.

BARBARA'S STORY

Barbara's guiding verse is:

"In all your ways acknowledge him, and he will make your paths straight" (Proverbs 3:6).

She added, "Even when I am not sure where I want my path to go."

Barbara made a late decision to join a tour to the Middle East and Europe. She knew one person on the tour, and that person became her good roommate. In Switzerland, about halfway through the tour, a tour member who was a widower, asked Barbara to take a walk with him.

"That was the beginning of a friendship that I thought would end with the summer tour," she said. "Not so! We were married the following June. No regrets. God is so good and delights in filling our cups with joy overflowing."

7.
WHICH CHURCH?

Since Omar was a pastor, I willingly went with him to his church and even had my membership transferred there. However, this church was 26 miles from where we lived, and Omar's idea of being a pastor did not fit with living so far from the church. He resigned from there about seven months after our wedding. We decided to attend a church near our home, but, as it turned out, we were asked to come to a different church, about five miles away, and Omar accepted the call to be pastor there. I missed my home church, but it was not difficult to change. I soon made friends and felt a part of our new church family.

✻   ✻   ✻

It made good sense for Audrey to go to Jonathan's church since it was only a mile from where they lived, and her church was 26 miles away. His church was of the same denomination and conference as hers, so the move was not difficult for her.

For Evelyn, it was a little different because she belonged to one denomination and Frank, her husband-to-be, belonged to another. When they talked with her bishop before they got married, she said, "Oh Marvin, with Frank being a bishop in his church, I guess I'll have to leave mine. Marvin told her in his kindly way, "Evelyn, you have no choice. You belong with your husband. But," he added, "you'll always belong to your people at heart."

Joyce found leaving her church and the place where she had her roots to be one of her hardest adjustments. "I felt close to my church," she says, "and I really miss that. But my husband doesn't mind if I go back and do things with my friends. In fact, he encourages me to go." He had asked her before they married, "How do you feel about going to another church?" She thinks that if she had realized what his church was like, she might not have gone there. "It's certainly Christian," she says, "but I was brought up in a church where I was part of a regular Sunday School class. I got to know a group of women well. But then," she concludes, "I wouldn't want to go to a different church from my husband."

Eileen's husband had been brought up in one denomination, but later his family changed to a different one. During premarital counseling, the pastor gave some introduction to Eileen's church, which her husband-to-be joined. They were married there.

Fran belonged to one denomination and her husband belonged to another. She did not want to alternate between churches as some do, so she joined her husband's church. "It took a while til I felt I belonged—and til I felt accepted," she says.

"For a while," says one second wife, "I kept my membership where I had been a lifelong member, and we sometimes went to my church. But because he was so involved in his church, I thought it was better for me to transfer my membership there. It was not a difficult move since we were both in the same denomination and conference."

Amy and her husband-to-be dated for a while, but they broke up mainly because they couldn't agree on a church, and she did not want a divided house. Later, when they talked again, he was willing to visit different churches to see if they could agree on a church. When they found a church they both felt good about, Amy was ready to marry him.

Marcia and Bruce both belonged to the same denomination, but different conferences. She went to his church and it was no problem for her. "We didn't think it was good," she says, "to uproot young children from their church."

"Bruce was a deacon in the church," Julie says "so of course, I went to his church."

For one second wife, church attendance became a huge problem. She and her husband came from different denominations, and before marriage they decided to each leave their churches and to go together to a different church. But he only went with her a couple of times before marriage, and after marriage he said, "If you think I'm going back to that church, you've got another thought coming. We're going to my church when I say, and if I don't go you don't go." This was only one problem in a severely troubled marriage.

Susan had been active at her church, and George was still preaching once a month or so at his. So she went with him there. "It felt to me like going to a strange church," she recalls.

"But I have adjusted to it. We go back to my church several times a year."

Annette and Abner belonged to different churches in the same district, which are about 15 minutes apart. They go back and forth and feel that each has absorbed a whole new church full of friends instead of dropping one.

Roger had been in one church for the last 20 years; Rosene belonged to a different denomination. They went back and forth for a while and made it a big prayer concern while agonizing over the decision. His trusted missionary friend told Roger not to worry, that God would take care of it. His friend was right. Rosene and Roger were both willing to go to the other's church. After a couple of months, Roger started feeling a bit distant from his church and increasingly comfortable at her church. The people in her church made him feel very welcome. Rosene recalls, "We had people say we should both break away from our churches and go to another one. But now, especially with a new minister coming in, we are together in this new beginning; he will be 'our' minister."

CHERYL'S STORY

Cheryl recalls that near the end of her 27 years of missionary service in Miami, she thought someone stood by her saying, "Well done, thou good and faithful servant." It was so real that she answered out loud, "Yes." She knew she had completed God's time in Miami and her future was "back home."

Saying good-bye to job and church family was difficult. "They didn't want me to leave," she recalls, "but after I explained that I sensed God guiding me, they accepted my call to move on. With mixed feelings I left my Florida home for Pennsylvania. It is really amazing how God put all the pieces of the puzzles together—a place to live, a job, and a church family."

Cheryl says she was content in her single life and new environment, when a phone call changed her life. "A gentleman whom I never knew asked me to share a meal with him. I was so excited I didn't know what to do. I needed time to think, so I told him to call me in two weeks."

Finally, they met at a restaurant and became acquainted during a delightful evening. He asked to see her again and she said, "Yes." He had been married for 30-plus years and his wife was deceased, so now he was lonely and needed a friend. "We enjoyed being together, and our friendship developed rapidly," she says. "Our relationship flowed into his family of six children and their spouses and his grandchildren. It all seemed so natural. God moved in helping me with my future plans, and I had no fear, because I believed God was in control. To be a grandmother felt good to me.

"The best moment in my life was when he asked me to become his wife. What peace."

To prepare for this big step meant, once again, a round of good-byes for Cheryl—to her job, landlord, and so on. It was a sad, but happy time. Cheryl and her husband chose a motto for their journey: "We are climbing life's stairway together."

8.
MONEY
AND VALUES

Omar and I had a lawyer draw up a prenuptial agreement and new wills for each of us. On the day of our wedding we signed the wills and had them witnessed. The lawyer found our wills to be a challenge—not the usual boilerplate documents.

For our everyday operations, we put our money into one checking account in both names. Yes, we managed with one checkbook for household and personal expenses. We used a budget, recorded expenditures, and trusted each other, keeping no secrets about what we did with money. We gave each of us a small amount of cash each month that we did not need to give account of. It went on the budget as spent for allowances. Then we had a separate checkbook for the "Lord's Account," where we deposited a certain percentage of our incomes and decided together when, where, and how much to give. We both feel comfortable with this method and enjoy having money to give.

Both of us were brought up in families where money was scarce, and we learned to be frugal. Before we were married we discussed finances. I think Omar was a bit scared I might spend money too freely, and I wondered if he would be tight with money. But it didn't take long for us both to be comfortable handling our money. I really felt a great freedom with the way we did finances.

The responses I received on money matters show that there are many different ways to handle finances.

One said, "We put our money together and have both names on all our accounts."

A couple who both grew up during the Depression and have similar values feel comfortable with joint accounts.

Another couple puts their accounts together except for monies earning interest.

One very independent person had controlled the finances in her first marriage. When she explained that to her second husband, he said that's what he liked about her. His first wife had been extremely dependent, and he was happy to have a wife who would take charge of finances. They put their money together, except for her Social Security check, and she takes care of paying the bills.

On the other hand, some chose to keep separate accounts but share living expenses. Being older and having established patterns of using money, these couples find this works best for them.

One couple divides their expenses this way: The husband takes care of household expenses and food. She buys her own clothes, pays her medical bills, car expenses, and other personal items. If there is something she wants for the house that he does not think is necessary, she gets it with her own money.

In one couple, the woman married an older widower and she didn't have much money of her own, so her husband pays the household expenses. She uses her own money for special things—holidays, Christmas gifts, personal items, charitible giving, and so on.

Being single and independent for many years, one second wife found it difficult to pool her finances with her husband's. He is very frugal, and she enjoys sharing her money. So he pays all the household expenses, and she's in charge of vacations and recreation! Being the last surviving member of her family, she inherited more money than her husband, so she has more to spend on gifts and extras, and she loves it.

Another couple left their individual savings and investments accounts each in their own names, but they put their present incomes into a joint checking account to use for their living expenses. She keeps the records and pays the bills, and both are happy with the arrangement. Both of them had big families, grew up on farms, and share a reluctance about spending for luxuries.

In another situation the husband is more generous and believes in buying quality, while the wife is more frugal.

Although they put their money together, one second wife says she felt scared about it. She didn't want to have to ask her husband for money for every little thing. She recalls that her mother even needed to ask her father for a nickel for a candy bar. The solution? Her husband offered to give her an allowance. Now she has some money to spend all by herself which she doesn't need to account for. They have joint ownership on all their accounts, but they have two checkbooks for their joint checking account. He does the bookkeeping, and it is working out well for them.

Another second wife says that she and her husband didn't talk about money before they got married. She didn't have a lot of money, but the little she had saved she kept in a separate account. Her generous husband paid all the expenses and saw to it that she was well provided for after his death.

Still another woman says that she and her husband did not discuss finances before marriage. She feels this was wrong, but in their case it all worked out. After they built a new home, and still had not drawn up wills, her husband died suddenly of a massive heart attack. It could have been a real fiasco, but the estate was settled without a hitch. The lawyer said he never had an estate with so many people involved be executed with so few problems. The family said, "To God be the glory."

One second wife feels that it was a mistake to have put all their money together, a failure of not having received proper counseling. They each have children. When they later divided their accounts, it was very difficult. Now they have a joint checking account into which they each enter the same amount each month. They pay their living expenses from this joint account, but keep their other monies separate.

The way a couple handles money depends somewhat on who has money and how much. Since in one case the man's income is considerably higher than his wife's, he pays most of the monthly bills, and she chips in with groceries when they entertain her friends. She also does her part by paying for the things that "make a house a home" —bedding, towels, tablecloths, pictures, lamps, decorative goods, and so on. She pays for all of her personal items, all of her own clothing, and much of his clothing. They often split the cost of eating out.

A husband who loves to travel, and takes an extensive trip almost every year, asked his second wife to pay half of the trip the first year they traveled together. As time went on, he saw she was not "out to spend all his money," and didn't really have the money for all this travel, so now he pays for the trips. She buys the souvenirs, if any, pays for the film and pictures they take, and picks up the tab for an occasional meal. Nice motel rooms mean more to her than to him, and sometimes she'll pay the difference for an upgrade!

For one woman who married after retirement age, "It was sweet music to my ears that my husband wanted me to keep my own money." She never expected to live rent-free and receive free groceries and gas, but she thoroughly enjoyed it.

Another couple keeps separate accounts, but the wife deposits all but a monthly allowance of about $150 from her present income into her husband's bank account. Income from her investments and property remains in her estate.

One young single believed that her husband-to-be had a lot of money. When they discussed it, she learned that he thought all single women have a lot of money. They found out that neither of them had as much money as the other thought! She says, "We got married anyway!" They put all their money together and worked things out to each one's satisfaction.

Another young single who married a widower found that money was not a problem, even though she was in Christian service for most of her single years and didn't have much. He wanted her to sell her car because he had one, and then he got a truck for himself. Getting rid of her own car was hard for her.

In a situation where a widower with nine children married a 26-year-old, and they then had two more children, they put their money together. He willed his estate to her. When she dies, the estate will go equally to all the children—his and theirs.

Another did it this way: "What each of us had earned and saved or inherited before marriage remained in our individual names. What we earned and received after our marriage we put into our combined account."

One couple has a joint checking account in addition to their separate checking accounts. The wife thinks it would be hard for her not to have her own account, which allows her both freedom and control. They keep their investments separate, but they know each other's finances and keep no secrets.

Money was never a problem for one widow with children who married a widower with children. Her new husband encouraged her to keep her own checking account. They also had a joint account. His attitude was that money is to be spent. He was not a penny-pincher and trusted her, never questioning why she spent what she did. They kept their estates separate for tax purposes.

One second wife says her husband continues to extend a life insurance policy and monthly savings account that takes effect if he departs before she does.

A lawyer was concerned that one woman's future would be looked after, since she gave up years of earning potential. Her husband is making some provision for her in his will, and he started an annuity for her with a down payment. She makes the ongoing quarterly payments.

One husband has made financial provisions for his wife to go to a retirement home if he dies first.

One couple sought advice from a financial counselor. His lawyer drew up an agreement and her attorney examined it. Then the two lawyers went over it and worked it out so that the wife has the lifetime right to live in the house her husband owns. As an alternative, she may sell the house and use the money to go to a retirement home if she chooses. There is also a trust whereby she will have income for the rest of her life after he passes away. She will get interest on the principal until her assets are depleted, and then she can draw from the principal of the trust. They have also taken out long-term care insurance.

One couple set up a testamentary trust with each other as the beneficiary.

A couple who each brought young children into the new family said they fully aired the subject before marriage. They keep their finances separate now, mainly because of the children. She gets social security for the children. They split up their expenses and it works well. They are both generous and don't feel that either one is taking advantage of the other.

※ ※ ※

Regarding wills, one woman who had no children of her own had willed a portion of her assets to her sister's children who were special to her. Now she and her husband, by mutual consent, have decided to keep it that way.

Another woman who had no children, and married a man with grown children, decided not to will her previously-saved money to her nieces, nephews, nor to her stepchildren, since she feels they all appear to have sufficient.

Another has willed most of her assets to charity. Her stepchildren are well taken care of by her husband's will.

In her earlier will, one woman gave her estate to her brothers and sister, to missions, and to schools. Her new will remains the same, except that, because her husband has a trust for her, she has included his children in her will.

Another has included "her" grandchildren in her will.

Another gave some money she inherited from her family to her brothers and sisters. Her lawyer said it would be appropriate for her to give more than that to her family, but in her situation it seemed right to will the rest to her deceased husband's children.

One has willed money to a sibling and nieces and nephews, as well as to her stepchildren.

Another says that after she married, the change in her will was mostly just a name change.

In a case where a couple kept their investments separate, the second wife has willed her investments to her stepchildren and a few other beneficiaries. Her reason for not willing it to her nieces and nephews is that none of them live closeby, and she feels that it will be the stepchildren who will help her in her later years.

A single woman, who married a widower with children ages 14, 11, and four, says, "We put our money together. If there is money left someday, it will go to our children, for indeed his children became our children the day we married. They called me Mother or Mom from that day on, and I love them as my own."

In an updated will, one second wife made a list of some of her furniture and pictures which should go to her nieces. But she thought that if she had done this a few years later, she might have willed some things to grandchildren who now seem like hers and who didn't know their first grandmother.

One who is a widow for the second time reports that her second husband willed his estate to be divided among his and her children equally, and she receives his retirement benefit. Her will provides for all of the children, his and hers, to receive equal shares from her estate.

In a situation where both spouses had children from previous marriages, his will gives everything to her for as long as she lives, and then it goes to his children, while her children are willed the money and assets she had prior to her second marriage.

Gathered Wisdom

1. Be sure to look carefully at finances before your marriage. Talk about values; go shopping together; learn to know each other's spending habits.
2. It is important in a second marriage to have a prenuptial agreement drawn up by a lawyer. Attorneys generally recommend a prenuptial agreement for everyone, even first marriages.
3. Keep a budget and record all expenditures. Trust each other completely, keeping no secrets from each other regarding finances.
4. Many wives who are not, or have not been, the primary wage-earners, still like to enjoy some independence in spending money. A woman can arrange for this, either by keeping her own checking account, or by budgeting an allowance for herself which she does not have to give an account of.
5. The important thing is not how many checking accounts you have, or whether assets are in both names or separate, but that you both agree, trust each other, and feel comfortable and satisfied with the arrangement. Be sure to have the ultimate plans for distribution of the assets in writing.
6. Both of your wills should be written before the wedding and signed right after the ceremony.
7. Where there are children and stepchildren, the will should determine the fair distribution of all assets. If both spouses have children, each will most likely will their separate estates to their own children.
8. A woman with no children who marries a widower with children may decide to will the assets she accumulated prior to marriage to her siblings or nieces and nephews. Who inherits her assets may depend in part

on how close she has been to her stepchildren, siblings, and nieces, and nephews. Her wishes should be
in writing and should be fair to all.

9. Long-term care insurance can protect assets for heirs,
but it is not wise for everyone. Check with a financial
counselor to see if it is an affordable option for you.

10. Financial affairs can be very flexible. There are no pat
answers. Each couple should work out their own solution.

ELVA'S STORY

As a young girl, Elva wanted to find a good Christian husband, but she did not want to be a farmer's wife, and most of the young men she knew were farmers. So after dating many good men, Elva decided to pursue a career. She worked in the textile industry, and eventually she was transferred to a New York office. She worked for the company nearly 40 years, 20 of them in the city. She found her work and the city interesting and enjoyable. Then . . .

One evening Elva returned to her home area to speak at a fund-raising dinner for a city camp which she supported, and she stopped at her home enroute to the banquet hall.

"My mother handed me a letter," she said. "And when I saw the return name and address I guessed what the contents might hold. I was not at all interested in reading it. My mother and I continued to the dinner without my saying a word about it.

"When I arrived back in New York at about three in the morning, I opened the letter and read it. It was just what I had suspected, and my reaction was to scrap it and forget it. The writer started the letter by introducing himself, and then mentioned that he had recently lost his wife and found himself alone. He said he asked the Lord what he should do with his life now. His many friends told him he was too young to stay single and even gave him suggestions. He said my name kept coming to him, even though he had no idea about what had become of me.

"After much prayer and thought, he decided to write a letter, but since he had no idea where to send it, he put it in a stamped, sealed envelope, and then wrote a short note to my parents asking them to forward it."

Elva truly wanted to scrap the letter, but when she reread it she thought, Anyone who wants the Lord's will for his life needs a reply.

Even though she returned to her home area every weekend, Elva felt confident that this old farmer would not come to New York. So she simply wrote that she lived in the city, and that she was very happy, had a lucrative job, and was quite satisfied. She told him that she too wanted the Lord's will for her life. "I felt quite safe," she said, "in saying I would have dinner with him if he came to New York. (His son-in-law said to her later, 'You didn't know Dad, did you?')

"He promptly replied that I should give him a date and place where we could meet, and he would be there! I had no out. So I gave him a date six weeks in the future because I was busy."

The farmer came to New York, they met at the appointed place, and they had a nice dinner and evening together. "He then suggested that because of the distance he might stay for the weekend and that we could spend Sunday together, too. So he stayed in a hotel downtown and met me the next morning. We went to church together and had dinner. After a pleasant afternoon, he asked if he could see me again."

At this point Elva decided to ask a few questions. She asked about his children, and he told her he had six sons and one daughter, all married. She immediately said, "Not interested!" (She had always prayed that she would never have or be a stepmother.) He promptly assured her that his children would not object, especially since they had their own homes. That didn't satisfy Elva. She said she would not see him again unless he talked to each child about his idea of another companion.

Again he came through and did what she thought might stop him. He told her that all except one said, "Dad, you are too young to stay single; we have our families; it would be all right."

Elva said, "But the one! What did he say?"

"His reply was, 'Dad, you did a good job when you chose my mother. I know you will do a good job again.'"

Now what was I to do? I had a good job which I enjoyed, I had my parents and a home to go to anytime, I had good health, I had everything going for me. Did I dare to venture into this relationship and take a risk?

She prayed, "Lord, what should I do?" The courtship continued for about a year, with positive affirmations from many, including her parents. He was a farmer, living in a rural area. She lived in a major city, having never lived in the country. But after she met all the children and grandchildren and other related families . . . "You *guessed it! We had a lovely wedding. I left my job in the city, moved to the farm, and have had a great life." She says, "My final thought is, 'When you are in the Lord's will, you can't go wrong or be unhappy.'"*

9.
CHILDREN
AND STEPCHILDREN

*O*mar tells me that one thing he considered important in choosing a second wife was to find someone who would relate well to his children. (Now I call them *our* children.) Rachel chose to live with us for a while. She and I were quite different in many ways, as, for example, when we worked together in the kitchen. While I was still studying the recipe, Rachel had everything mixed up ready for the oven. We had many good times together and came to be friends and love each other. It took longer to get acquainted with John Daniel, since he was away at college and was with us for only short periods of time. But now I feel a strong bond of friendship with him and dearly love him, his wife, and our two precious grandsons. J.D. and Rachel both call me Martha, which is fine with me. I feel more like a friend than a mother to them.

✳ ✳ ✳

Most of the women I interviewed related good experiences with children and stepchildren. Most children accepted their new mother, and many were glad their father had someone to be happy with again after his loss. Of course, there were difficulties, too. The women I interviewed shared these experiences:

Stepmothers Accepted

Jewel wishes everyone would be as fortunate as she in respect to stepchildren. The friend who introduced the couple to each other told Jewel before she even met her husband-to-be, "You won't have any objection from his children—they want him to marry again." They received her warmly into their family. His daughter even offered to make Jewel's wedding dress. All of the children have made frequent trips from Canada to stay with them in Pennsylvania and in Florida, and they buy her Mother's Day gifts. The children call her Jewel, and the grandchildren call her Grandma. "I think the contacts between the two families got off to a healthy start," Jewel says, "when his children had a 'Trousseau Tea' for us in Canada before our marriage." This Canadian tradition was an open house for the community to come and meet her and her family.

* * *

Susan's children were all with her at her daughter's house when George called. He told her he was lonesome and that his wife had died several months before. Her children thought it was great, except for the daughter with whom she lived, but when she met George it was fine with her, too.

His children had said to him, "Daddy, did you ever think about re-marrying?" Each of his children has thanked Susan for coming into their father's life and making him so happy.

✳ ✳ ✳

Beulah says, "The children were all happy about our marriage. His daughter said, 'Well, Daddy, there just is nobody else.'"

His children call her Aunt Beulah, an affectionate name she was called when they were both at the same mission location many years earlier and had known each other. Beulah recalls, "His daughter and my daughter had been in school together and used to say they wished they could be sisters. Now they are!"

✳ ✳ ✳

Audrey didn't know any of Jonathan's children or grandchildren. They were all married and out of the nest before she dated Jonathan. When she met them at Christmas-time, she decided on the maxim, "Don't be sharp. Don't be flat. Be natural." That's the way it's been. As the children and grandchildren were introduced at the wedding reception, many of the children got up and spoke words of appreciation for Audrey in front of the more than 200 guests.

✳ ✳ ✳

Stella told her husband-to-be, "I really want to know how the children feel about me." She soon had an opportunity to meet them on a weekend get-together. She says, "We were all a little crazy, and I thought I would fit in!" Soon after she met the children he proposed. "They've been great," she says.

✳ ✳ ✳

Elva, who was married only a short time before her husband died, says regarding her stepchildren, "We are very close and always have great times together. Whenever, wherever, or whatever the occasion, they are always ready to cooperate and have fun."

❋ ❋ ❋

Cheryl says, "With open hearts and minds, the children accepted me; I could feel it! Their father helped to prepare them for this change, and even their mother had spoken to them about this possible future change."

❋ ❋ ❋

Pat learned that the daughter of her husband-to-be had written to him and said that she wanted him to marry someone who was happy and a good listener, with whom they could talk about their problems. That felt like good news for Pat.

❋ ❋ ❋

In Amanda's case, her nieces and nephews became her stepchildren since she married her deceased sister's husband. She knows them well and enjoys a close relationship with them.

❋ ❋ ❋

Amy's first meeting with her future stepson was a tense one. When her husband-to-be was invited to his son's home for dinner, he didn't tell his son and his wife that he was bringing Amy. Amy feels this was not good, but later they were able to chuckle about it. Amy was only married 20 months and 10 days when her husband died. "During their father's illness, his family was so glad I was there," she says. Since his death, Amy is not sure how much to hold onto his children. "I don't want to disappear, but I don't want to force myself on them," she says.

Glad for Their Father's Sake

Abner's children had seen their father in the depth of despair after a series of traumatic events—a stroke, the death of his first wife, a heart attack, open heart surgery, and then rejection by a woman he wanted to marry. When Abner's children met Annette with him, they all agreed that they would accept a person who could make their father as happy as they saw him that day

* * *

The children graciously made Elaine feel a part of the family. One daughter, at her own wedding, said she would have liked to have her own mother with her for this special occasion, but since that was not possible, she was glad that Elaine could be there. Another daughter told Elaine in a written note that she felt Elaine was an answer to prayer for her and her dad, and was so thankful for her. The daughter did not want to be her dad's caretaker (she meant that kindly) and wanted to move on in her life. But she did not want him to be left alone. These affirmations meant so much, especially at a time when Elaine struggled with feelings of wanting to fit in and not quite knowing how. At times she felt she really did not do well. "But," she says, "today there is a wonderful relationship with the children and the family, and I'm so thankful for that blessing.

* * *

One second wife says her new husband's daughters were relieved when she married their father. She reflects, "I think we have a good relationship, although I don't always think the way they do. A friend of mine, who is also a second wife, and I have this little joke between us. We both have two stepdaughters. We say they're good to us and we enjoy being with them, but when the two of them are together they don't know we are there. They just talk and talk and talk with each other.

Fran observed that the children of her husband-to-be loved their father, and she knew that they favored his remarriage. It was his son who introduced him to Fran "because his father was lonely."

"When I met the children," Fran says, "I knew they had good parents, and I felt safe getting into the family. When you marry, you marry the man's family."

Laura says that before they married, her husband-to-be discussed marriage with his children and with his in-laws. He also had each child meet Laura. He invited her to attend a service at his church, too. She says, "The children have been very kind to me and have sent me beautifully worded Mother's Day cards, stating much appreciation for all I have done for their father. They seldom have mentioned their mother to me."

What to Call Her

Rebecca says, "Edwin's children are so good to me. The day of our wedding, when they came through to greet us, they said, 'Rebecca, may we call you Mom?'" It nearly floored her to be asked that question at the wedding. She told them, "If you feel comfortable calling me Mom, I'll accept it, but I wouldn't ask it of you." They call her Mom.

✳   ✳   ✳

Julie says, "It is an adjustment to have stepchildren; we have two at home yet, but they have accepted me well. The stepchildren don't call me Mom, and I didn't expect them to. I knew their mother and I don't feel worthy of that!"

✳   ✳   ✳

Myrtle is only 11-12 years older than her oldest stepchildren, and she feels more like one of them than like their mother. She and the oldest daughter phone each other every weekend or more often, and she calls the rest of the children periodically. One calls her Mom, but the rest knew her as their teacher. As one of them said, "It seems awkward since we were friends." She knew them and their mother for a long time prior to marrying their father. The children wanted to both laugh and cry at the wedding, since it was so soon after their mother died. "We talk freely about their mother," Myrtle says, "whom I knew well as a friend."

✳   ✳   ✳

Norma says her stepchildren have been kind and accepting of her. They call her by her first name, which is fine with her, and the grandchildren call her Grandma. Norma says, "I believe my daughter felt the need for a father, and she chose to call my new husband Dad."

Grandchildren

One of the grandchildren didn't want her grandpa to have anybody take the place of Grandma. But she likes Annette, and they get along fine now. One of his daughters was a bit leery, too, at first, but after the third time together she told Annette that she accepts her. "I think," said Annette, "she realized I was not trying to take the place of her mother."

"One weekend," Julie says, "our three grandchildren were staying with us, and the three-year-old asked me, 'Are you my daddy's mommy?' I said, 'No, his mommy died when you were a little baby, only two weeks old.' My husband heard our conversation and came to my rescue, explaining to his grandson that Grandmommy had died and gone to heaven, and that then he married me! Later, the child asked me, 'Grandma, how does Grandpa know everything?'"

Eileen says of her husband's children, "They're wonderful and make me feel that I belong. I love them, and the grandchildren who never knew their first grandmother are extra special to me."

Vera married young, and she and her husband had two children of their own. "Our youngest is only 2½ years older than our oldest grandchild," she says. "Our two boys love the grandchildren. Now we have 10 grandchildren. They each call me Grandmother, and each one is special. This is one of the crowning points of marrying a widower. I didn't have to wait long for grandchildren. They started coming when I was 38!"

Elaine says she is not a person with lots of creative ideas about how to relate to and do things with grandchildren, and she finds that quite frustrating. She and her husband enjoy taking their 14 grandchildren to a cabin at a camp for several days. This has proven to be a positive and enjoyable time both for the grandchildren and their parents (who love the free time). "We go through a lot of food," she says, "and we go at a high energy level from early in the morning to late at night! At the end of the stay we and the grandchildren are exhausted, but we have survived, treasuring many wonderful and precious memories."

✳ ✳ ✳

Bertha's husband counseled with each of his children about marrying again. They respect Bertha and are thankful their father has a home and that their children have a grandmother. At the suggestion of one of the grandchildren, they call her Grandma Bertha.

✳ ✳ ✳

Even though her husband isn't living anymore, Rhoda keeps up good contact with his children. She has invited the grandchildren and their spouses together for a meal. They appreciated it so much that she wants to do it every year.

✳ ✳ ✳

Two of Pat's young grandchildren said, "Grandma, why do you have to get married?" They liked her house, the things they had there to play with, the paths in her garden. But she fixed a room in her new home and explained that it was for them—with their favorite sofa, table, games, stuffed toys, and Cabbage Patch dolls. And when they met her husband, they liked him and are now content with their grandmother and new grandfather.

Timing

Sylvia says, "'Our' children were in their forties when we married, and they have been wonderful to me. But," she says, "if I had to do it over again, I'd have waited a longer time between their mother's death and the announcement of our engagement, because it was a blow to my husband's daughter. We are all Christians and we try to practice Christ's love, but I'd recommend to others in a similar situation that they *slow down*. His children and I had never met, either, so I was really a bolt out of the blue!"

Showing Affection

Her new husband still had two college-age children at home (and four married children) when Barbara and he married. "I felt it important to ease into the wife/homemaker role and not to try to change routines or furnishings," she says. "It was hard for the family to lose their mother and adjust to this new wife." She didn't expect them to call her Mother, but she says it has felt good to be called Grandma. She remarks, "Why wouldn't they be uncomfortable seeing their father show affection to a second wife? We tried not to make them uncomfortable. Change and loss take time to heal."

❋ ❋ ❋

"My husband knew he had to be careful when he showed affection to me," Pat says, "on account of his children."

❋ ❋ ❋

"We don't show much affection in front of the children, except good-bye kisses, and they don't seem to mind that. I think they expect that. One change for his children was my calling their daddy Honey. One time or so I heard his daughter calling him Honey, just teasingly. That seemed to sound strange to them. My husband said he used to call his first wife Mom. He calls me Honey most of the time, but it was an adjustment for him."

* * *

Sylvia reflects, "If the children were uncomfortable seeing their father be affectionate with me, they never showed it! In fact, his daughter once said during her father's beloved football game, 'Put your arm around Sylvia and pretend she's the football, Dad!' She came a long way in four hours the day we first met, and she's very special, as they all are."

* * *

When Marie married, her husband had three children at home, ages 14, 11, and four. She continued to work at her job, but her mornings and evenings were busier. The children accepted her well. "I just seemed to belong there," she says. "I never think of them as stepchildren. They are like my own. I don't think the children were uncomfortable about seeing Bob show affection to me. They often saw us hug and kiss. Bob felt it was important that they see us do this, especially since we both came from homes where our parents didn't do this around the family."

* * *

Elaine and her husband never displayed a lot of affection around the children and tried to be sensitive to their feelings. A new person had come into their home, and they needed to adjust to that. It was a difficult time for them involving many emotions. They were happy for their father in his marriage, but at the same time they grieved for their mother. With another person in their lives and in their father's life, they were experiencing lots of changes. Grief does not come in neat little packages and go away in a year or two. It has a lot of faces. Elaine encourages the children to be free to talk about their mother. "I do not feel threatened by her," she says. "She was their life and will always be their mother."

Difficulties

Being a stepmother was more of an adjustment for Vera than she expected. She found it hard to talk personally with the children. "It was a real challenge," she says, "to adjust to marriage with the children around and looking on, and with our needing to relate to them at the same time. A stepmother needs to be very unselfish." She sensed that the children still wanted their own mother and were adjusting to the fact that she would never come back. Vera worked through a lot of the feelings with them, but it was not easy.

When the two oldest children learned that Vera was expecting a baby, they found it hard to accept. Vera and her husband decided beforehand to have only two children together in order to respect the older children's feelings. Furthermore, her husband was already 40 when they got married, and the two older children were 15 and 18. Vera says of her own two boys, "I find them much easier to communicate with. Not that they are any better behaved, but we can express our feelings and clear the air so much easier."

✳ ✳ ✳

Elaine found that she needed to get rid of many assumptions she held as a single person, about what it would be like living in a family with teenagers. She learned quickly that their place in life's cycle and her place were two different worlds. She says, "I knew all this in my head, but when the reality of it emerged, I needed to stretch and adjust, and it was not always easy." For example, she expected cooking to be a breeze because she enjoyed entertaining. She hadn't counted on the different tastes of pizza-age children!

Elaine also found it frustrating to cope with different personalities, especially when they were so different from hers. One daughter expressed her thoughts and emotions freely, making it easy to know her opinions and feelings. Elaine wished she could do the same. However, she tended to hold her feelings in, with the result that no one really knew what she was thinking until her feelings burst out.

One of Elaine's priorities, and, she admits, excessively so, was keeping things orderly. This was not important for one of the daughters. Elaine says, "I am not being critical in saying this; we simply had different emphases about what mattered most, and at times this created conflicts.

Elaine needed to learn to give and to be more open, and she feels she did not always do that well. Because she entered a strong family unit, she thinks that both the married children and the two daughters at home adjusted more easily and freely than she did. Today one of the daughters is in the medical profession and uses her wonderful personality and disposition to relate to a wide range of people. Elaine says, "She taught me that some things just don't matter all that much. We all have our own priorities, unique to each one of us, and as we blend and work together it brings caring and love into the family. These things don't all fit together like a puzzle; instead it takes a lot of giving and loving." Elaine realizes, "I needed to learn to accept or overlook others' ways of doing things."

The other daughter who was still at home has a personality which in some ways is more similar to Elaine's. Both girls were easy-going, and Elaine says, "I needed to learn not to be so rigid and to become more flexible." She admired both daughters' ability to swing with the punches and not get stressed out over little things.

Another challenge for Elaine had to do with the fact that one of the daughters in the family had functioned as mother to the younger children during their mother's illness and death. This daughter has the personality, instinct, and ability for this role, and she did it well. She and her siblings grew up together, played together, and bonded together, and in their mother's death this bond became even stronger. This stability carried them through the hard times. "As a stepmother," Elaine says, "I found it difficult to know how and where to fit into this, especially with my preconceived ideas of how families function. At times I felt left out and inadequate, but I came to realize that their family ties are strong, and in this situation it was the normal route to be taken. It was nothing personal against me. Bonding, and a lifestyle that had developed with the death and illness of their mother, did not need to change now, especially since they are grown children."

"A significant factor in building our relationship," Elaine told me, "was that my husband talked with the children about me before we were married and kind of took them along in our relationship, making them feel a part of us. A big adjustment for me was that when we were dating, for the most part it was he and I, and after marriage the 'we' became four people. I looked forward to being married, yet felt somewhat fearful about the role I would have in the family. After we were married, my husband worked hard at helping me understand what had shaped his children, and what had made me who I am. Through times of misunderstandings, tears, and tension, but also times of mending feelings, we moved on together."

✳ ✳ ✳

One second wife found having stepchildren difficult. "It's not like they're your own. They treat their dad well, and they include me in their gatherings. They've always been friendly and considerate." But she had to adjust to their different ways of doing things. "Like at the noon meal," she says, "sometimes it's one o'clock till we eat, and they'll all stand around and pick at the food before we sit down. It's not like I was used to where we'd all sit down to eat at the same time."

✳ ✳ ✳

Married at age 26, Marcia became mother to children ages one-and-a-half to 16, and found developing good relationships a challenge. "I wish I would have taken more time to understand them better," she reflects. "We had a dairy with 100 cows, the children helped in the barn, and the day was filled with work, work, work! I had meals to do, lunches to pack—it was a full-time job. By evening everybody was tired and often in bed by 8:30.

"Then we had three more children. I tried to watch and make sure that I didn't spend more time with my younger ones. As my stepchildren matured, they all accepted me, and now they are all really special, even though their father is no longer living. Every other year I reserve a place in the mountains—a big cabin—and invite all the children and grandchildren. Of course they cannot always all come, but we have a great time together."

✳ ✳ ✳

Maria, who married young and became a stepmother to six children, ages seven to 17, knows that some of the children felt uncomfortable seeing their father show affection to her, but others were glad. Maria and her husband had two daughters together, so then she had eight children to relate to. It was somewhat overwhelming for her, especially since her husband was an extremely hard worker with lots of energy. Even though she was 19 years younger, she found it hard to keep up. Now that her daughters are 11 and 12 years old, she says, "Without them I would have left this marriage and this house. I feel like a stranger in this family. The children of my husband's first marriage have a home here, but not his second wife."

Recently Maria and her husband have gotten help from a psychologist. Maria wanted to have a break from the visits of the children and grandchildren. Now they are resuming the visits, slowly, and feeling good about the relationships. She says, "The magic word in every relationship is *communication*. I have much to learn."

✳ ✳ ✳

Janette did not find her role to be easy. A couple of times she was told, "You're not my mom; you can't tell me what to do." She realized that the children had gone through severe trauma due to the way their mother died.

Her own children also had big adjustments. Her son came to his own wise conclusion as he said, "If my father were living, things would be different. But on the other hand, I don't know how it would be if he were living."

In adjusting, Janette went through learning, tears, and frustrations. She says, "There were times when I felt that for my husband, his children came before me. It seemed like I was doing all the giving in, and that it was time he did some giving in. I wanted him to learn to share his feelings. But when I gave up my need to make him talk, it wasn't such a big issue."

Those first years were difficult, but Janette is glad she didn't give up. She says, "The Lord led, not *out*, but *through*."

* * *

Phoebe had a teenage daughter, and her husband a teenage son still at home, which made their adjustment a bit difficult. Also a daughter in another state found it hard to think of her father in love with someone other than her mother, but when she met Phoebe and saw them together she felt good about it.

* * *

Cathy's husband and his first wife had no children, so even though Cathy was a second wife, she had no stepchildren. "But my being a second wife did cause some anxiety for our oldest son. When he was about seven years old, he came home from boarding school one weekend all upset about something. In trying to find out what was troubling him, we learned that someone at school had told him that I wasn't his mother. While we didn't plan to keep it a secret from our children that their father had been married before, we just hadn't told them yet. It didn't take long to clear that one up, but it did cause him some grief for a while."

* * *

Right after their wedding one second wife was told by her new husband that she was supposed to *pay* to take her husband's daughters along on their honeymoon to England. She said, "I'm not planning to take my children, and I'm not taking yours." On the honeymoon she knew she had made the biggest mistake of her life by marrying this man.

By Christmas she was a nervous wreck. Her children came to the Christmas dinner she made at his house. "It was the worst Christmas I ever had," she says. "He gave his children *a lot* and much less to mine. I was not supposed to spend money on my children. My children felt very uncomfortable in his home."

* * *

Rosene highlighted a common difficulty for mothers of blended families. "I feel as though I'm spread too thin to be a really good mother to anybody. It was a struggle to give up my dreams of close relationship with my two girls. Now I have four girls, and you can't have as close a relationship with four people as you can with two. My oldest daughter is quiet, and when our daughters come home from school, the other three are talking. She'll stand there a little bit and then drift off. So my relationship with her has really suffered because I don't have one-on-one time with her." But with her husband's teenage son, Rosene says she can't believe how easily she has slipped into a mother role. "He came to me and said, 'I hurt my wrist today.' He just wants some attention, like, 'Oh, I'm sorry.' That's what he needs."

It is a challenge for Rosene and Roger to find time for the two of them to be alone. They have a little time in the morning, but the children are up until 9:30 or 10:00 o'clock at night, and after that Rosene and Roger are both tired. Rosene says, "I'm so torn between all these children, and in my desperation to keep good relationships with them, I might put my relationship with Roger in second place." It takes a lot of emotional energy to be parents to seven children.

They do occasionally take time for a "date" and do something they both enjoy. "My husband," Rosene says, "is good at pushing for us to do things together." Even though it is a struggle for them to find quality time for the two of them, he understands her desire for that perfect relationship with all the children. He says, "If you'd look up the word 'mother' in Webster's Dictionary, you would see a picture of you, Rosene. You are one of the most natural mothers I have ever met."

Bonding

Rosene says, "The children may have adjusted more quickly than we did. They've been wonderful." She and Roger brought her four and his three together to have a new family of seven. Her youngest had the most difficulty. She says, "He still cries and doesn't like to live here. There aren't many children in this neighborhood like where we lived before." The oldest daughters in each family opted to room together, and they get along like genuine sisters. Rosene says, "I feel really good about how the children have adjusted, but I can see that the oldest ones are not going to say, 'He's my dad.' They call him Roger. And he doesn't expect them to call him Dad."

Both Rosene and Roger avoid the word "step." They never speak of a "stepson" or "stepdaughter." They always refer to our "son" or "daughter." They may use the term "original" if someone wants to know which are hers or his. "It's a little more friendly," they say. "We want to build a one-family unity here." Rosene credits Roger for that. "It's been one of his strong points, pulling everybody together, insisting that everybody must be treated alike. He'll say to them, 'your brother this,' or 'your sister that,' which sets an example for them."

❋ ❋ ❋

Annette and her husband took a course called, "Married and Loving it," in which they wrote love letters to each other and put them in sealed envelopes. After the course, the teacher mailed the letters to them. Now Annette's grown stepson wants his father and Annette to read those letters to the whole family at Christmas.

They all love Annette. She has done some interesting things to promote bonding with her husband's children and in-laws. She gave them each a "Questionnaire to help us know you better." They answered such questions as, Where do you work? What is your job title? What days/hours do you work? What colors do you really like? What foods do you dislike? What hobbies do you have? What music do you like? What makes you sad? . . . angry . . . happy and glad? What sports do you enjoy watching/playing? What places do you like to vacation? Your goals? Names you like to be called? And what name do you want us to sign on cards to you? Annette keeps these and refers to them on occasion. She also gave them a checklist which she titled, "Show Kids You Care," to help her know what kinds of responses from her they would interpret as caring for them.

* * *

One second wife was a bit uncomfortable with the little bit of gift-giving her husband did for his grandchildren. He gave them each $10 in cash at Christmas and sometimes on their birthdays. But she came from a family of extensive gift-giving and felt the grandchildren were somewhat cheated. But she also felt she didn't have the money to do much for so many grandchildren. She started out by giving each of them a Hallmark collectible Christmas ornament every year until they turned 18. Then to help celebrate her and her husband's tenth wedding anniversary, she took some personal money from savings and brought all 24 of his family together for a weekend. "We stayed in a motel with a pool and a family room," she says. "We visited tourist attractions and had wonderful family time. I guess I felt a weekend like that made up for the lack of gifts given at Christmas and birthdays and will probably be remembered longer than any gifts we've given."

* * *

Louise's role seemed more natural to her since she had had a stepmother. "Since I never had any children of my own, and I love my stepchildren dearly, they had more adjusting to do than I did. I told them I am here if they need me, I will not butt into their affairs, and I will mind my own business." She likes it if they ask her to do a bit of sewing or mending, or compliment her after she's made a meal, or when they feel free to take a pickle out of a dish as they pass the table before mealtime. "And the great-grandchildren are so precious," she says. "I love them all."

When widows marry widowers, and when both have grown children, the adjustment problems are not as difficult because the children are on their own and not immediately and constantly present at home.

When Thelma and Mark joined their two families, they had a total of 11 adult children. The dining room table seats 22, enough for Mark's family or her family, but they have not had them all at once in the three and a half years since they're married. Their children go to the same church, so they know each other, and Thelma hopes to have them all together at an outdoor picnic soon. Thelma feels accepted by Mark's children, and her children like Mark.

Helen's and her husband's families easily became one. Her one son and her husband's son were good friends before Helen was widowed. She says, "We had the affirmation of our families and friends, and we knew each other's backgrounds and extended families."

Fun and Humor

Elaine remembers, "As time went on, in spite of some difficult adjustments, we shared great family times and had a lot of fun together. The positive far outweighed the negative. Before our children went their separate ways to college, we took a family trip to the shore for two days and overnight. With a van and a tent, we packed ourselves together, ready for fun at a river inlet in Delaware. We arrived, pitched our tent, and went to the beach, all the time watching Hurricane Charlie come closer. Later that evening, as we returned to the river inlet, we were ordered to totally evacuate. We needed either to go to a local shelter or head back home. We decided to go home rather than 'shelter' it out. On the way we stopped for a snack. I couldn't believe how silly we were in the restaurant. I think everyone in our group enjoyed it, and other folks kind of entered into the fun—at 2:00 a.m.! Experiences such as this helped us grow and bond together."

Recalling another bit of humor, Elaine tells, "Early in our marriage the girls played a trick on me. People knew I liked cows, and so I got lots of cow items as gifts. The two girls were traveling, saw a cow calendar, and sent it to me. Well, I have many friends from the area they were visiting, and I automatically assumed it came from the group we call 'The Mountain Gang.' Our girls wouldn't 'fess up, and they got the biggest bang out of this as they kept egging me on. After quite some time my husband thought it was time for confessions, and I was totally shocked when they said they had sent it. I could not believe they had so skillfully pulled the surprise on me. It gave me a good feeling that they wanted to do something like that."

And then Elaine tells about another incident which was definitely not funny at the time, but turned out to be humorous. "One of the daughters placed her sneakers on the steps to take upstairs to her room. She carefully placed her keys in the heel of one of the sneakers, and yes, they were very visible. But when she carried the sneakers up the steps, the keys slid into the toe of her shoe. When she was ready to leave again, we searched, and we could not find those keys anywhere because she was not wearing those sneakers. Later, when she wore the sneakers and her toes found the keys, we could laugh about it."

Gathered Wisdom

1. In a second marriage it is not just the husband and wife who make adjustments, it is the children and the extended family as well. Adults cannot ignore their own needs, but they also need to reach out to the children.

2. Remember that no one can replace a mother.

3. Spend time, and try to strike up a relationship, with the children. At first you will want to spend time with your new spouse. This is a tension when the children are small—how to spend time with the children and have time alone with your spouse.

4. Keep up relationships with your new in-law families.

5. It may be helpful for the first wife's extended family to receive counseling about how to help her children work through the changes that come with being part of a new family. Sometimes these family members are still struggling with grief themselves and side with her children. It must be hard for them to see a new person taking their sister's place, but they can do a lot of damage or a lot of good, depending on their attitudes. They also need to accept the change, and to realize that the new mother is a unique person and will do things differently.

8. Learn not to be rigid and become more flexible. Recognize that when you are older—and marry—you will likely face challenges to some of your well-established patterns and preferences. Learn that most little things that bug you are not worth getting upset about.

9. Talk about your differences with your new spouse. Communication is so important!

10. Let the children talk to you about their deceased mother or father.

11. Don't insist that your stepchildren call you Mother. Let them call you what they feel comfortable with.
12. Compliment the children for things they help with at home.
13. Allow your spouse to be alone with his children, taking them out to eat, to hike, or just to spend time together at home.
14. Encourage your spouse to keep in contact with his and your married children who live far away.
15. When you come into a family, you anticipate becoming a part of all the joy and happiness of that family. Be aware that you *will* share in their sorrows and disappointments, too. That's life, and that's married life.
16. In times of death, divorce, or illness in your new family, the pain is unimaginable. You may wish for a degree in counseling or psychology. One second wife says, "Being a 'step,' I am slow to give counsel or opinions unless I am asked. But I have found myself in the role of a mediator, particularly when grown children go through a separation or divorce."
17. If they have difficulty working through the death of their mother, the children may need professional counseling. If their feelings are not dealt with, they can cause problems in later years.
18. Pray daily for the children and grandchildren, and hope that your marriage and love can be a model for them.
19. A second wife must be extremely flexible and unselfish. She needs to be prepared to take rejection without being offended and to learn to have fun and laugh with the children. At certain ages children may feel that they don't need to listen to her. Often it is not that they don't like the new mother, but that they just want their own mother back. Their emotions are on a roller coaster, and it takes them a while to work through things.

20. It is important to look at things from the other's viewpoint.
21. A second wife needs to be understanding of the children's feelings. It can be hard to communicate that you care and at the same time have authority. The children may not feel like listening, because they still want things to be like when their mother was there.

BERTHA'S STORY

Early in life Bertha had developed a conviction that she should be a missionary. Dan and his wife had already been in Africa five years before Bertha arrived to work with them. Dan called Bertha "Cousin" because he was a cousin to her father's first wife's children. So they knew each other within their extended families. In Africa Bertha helped Dan's wife during two pregnancies, including the time she gave birth to twin boys. Bertha took full care of the twins for a week while their mother was too weak to care for them. When Bertha returned to the United States, Dan and his wife had already been home a couple of years and they became neighbors. When Dan's wife lay dying in the nursing home, Bertha often stayed with her, and she was with her and some of the family when she died.

Soon after that, Dan accepted a three-year assignment in Africa. Before he left in October, he wrote Bertha a letter, asking if he could correspond with her while he was in Africa, and that if she agreed, he would like to see her before he left. And so, mutual friends invited both of them to their home for a meal. They went there separately, and after dark he brought her home but did not get out of the car. They met secretly in the home of these friends several times before he left.

Dan decided he wanted to announce their engagement at a missionary retreat in December, so he wrote and pro-

posed and asked her to answer in time for the retreat. She pondered over it and then wrote saying yes, but he didn't get her letter. So he called her and she gave him her answer. He announced it in Africa, and she was free to tell people, too.

Bertha says, "We got a lot of affirmation from friends and family, and everything seemed to fall into place." They did a lot of planning by letter and phone; then he came home so that they could get married in the spring. At the mission board's request, they spent two years together on an assignment in Africa.

10.
DIFFERENT AGES, DIFFERENT ENERGY LEVELS

Omar is a little more than four years older than I am. We belong to the same generation, both born in Depression years into families where money was scarce. After 23 years together, we still enjoy walking, traveling, and bird-watching, and we are active in church life. I feel fortunate to have a husband so near my age, and with whom I have so much in common.

✳ ✳ ✳

Most of the women who responded to my questions said that the age difference with their spouse has not been a problem. For several, though, marrying an older man created difficulties. One who at a young age married a man 19 years older, with six children still at home, says, "I was not much older than his children. I would never do it again. Now about 14 years later, he is a grandfather in his mind and thinking, and I am in my prime. It means we have a generation conflict!"

Joyce says it was good for her to marry an older, financially stable man. She believes the Lord sent her husband to her. Although she didn't have to worry much about money, she thinks that being 10 years apart in age is a little much, and says, "I hear him talking about things that happened when I was only 10 and he was 20. I think five years difference would be better."

* * *

Vera, who married 40-year-old Ben when she was 31, but looked even younger, did not consider age difference a problem between them, but it caused interesting reactions from other people. Vera says, "I was quite sensitive about this, especially when we were out in public as a family. I was only 13 years older than Ben's oldest son and didn't begin to look old enough to be his mother. It must have been confusing to people who didn't know us." She recalls, "One day a salesman came to the door and asked, 'Where is your Dad?' I told him in no uncertain terms that my *husband* was out in the barn!! He left rather quickly!" But Vera says the situation is alleviated now that the older children are married and since she has definitely aged faster than her husband in the past 18 years.

* * *

For a few of my friends, age difference made the decision to marry a difficult one. Evelyn, for instance, felt confident that the Lord brought Frank into her life. They met at garage sales and flea markets. She says, "I knew he was interested in me but was holding off out of respect since it was so soon after his wife had died." A year went by and they were still just talking. Evelyn wondered when he would ask her for a date. Finally she got a letter in which he asked to take her to a banquet. On their first date she found out how much older Frank was. That made her quite cautious. She had told her friends, "Don't let me ever marry a man 20 years older than I am."

When a good friend asked how her date went, she said, "We had a nice time, but I found out he is 10½ years older than I am. What do you say?"

"Go ahead," her friend answered. "That's not too big a difference." So she did, and the importance of their different ages faded as she realized how special he was to her. "I've been so thankful I married," she says, "especially since my parents died and I didn't have anyone—no brothers or sisters."

"In fact," Evelyn says, "now that we are older, he is kind of outdoing me. That's great. I'm glad he is so energetic."

It bothered Deborah at first that the man who asked her out was 21 years older than she. She said to him, "Pretty young, don't you think?" She says he didn't realize at the time that she was so much younger. In spite of his age, she is glad she consented to marriage. "He was a slower person than I," she says, "so we had to learn to give and take. I wanted to go places early, but it didn't always go that way. He was a man of ideas and creativity, and he encouraged me in my career."

Joanne married a man 23 years older than she is. He was persistent in getting her to date him in spite of her reluctance. He told her that when he thought about finding a second wife, it suddenly dawned on him, "Have you considered Joanne?" Later he wrote her a letter describing plans for a nice time together, but it didn't suit her for that day. She wrote back, but did not encourage him to pursue dating her.

A month or so later he wrote again, and she agreed to go out to eat together. She felt so at ease with him that she had the nerve to suggest another woman whom she thought more appropriate for him. "He knew my hang-up was our age difference," she says. "I didn't accept a second date that night."

After some weeks, still struggling, she agreed to go out to dinner again. "My decision to marry was not easy," she says, "but I soon found we had many similar interests, and I gradually came to peace about marrying him." At the time she was 44 and he was 67, but she says their energy level was alike, or that maybe he had more energy.

For Annette, an age difference of 18 years looked like too much for her at first. When a friend asked her if she might suggest her name to Abner, Annette said, "No." However, during the next week it seemed that God prepared Annette to think that if she got to know Abner, the age difference might not be a problem. She did not tell her friend about her change of mind, but Abner called her, and she accepted his invitation to go to a banquet with him. (She learned later that three people had given him her name within a two-week period!)

Annette had never met Abner before, and she wanted to get acquainted before they went out in public together, so she called him and asked him to come to her home. She says, "He did, and we spent four hours together, talking calmly as if we had known each other for years. We shared some personal things, and I cried as I shared with him about the death of my parents." (Annette learned later that this evidence of tenderness touched Abner, because he longed for a soul mate with whom he could share intimately.)

During that first time together Abner told Annette, "I had decided that I wanted a wife no more than 10 years younger than I am." But he came back in spite of their age difference.

Annette says that before she met Abner she had made a list of 24 characteristics which she wanted in a husband if God ever gave her one. It took her only five weeks to realize that Abner matched every point on her list, plus more. "If someone had told me when I was younger that I'd make up my mind in five weeks," she said, "I'd have said, 'I couldn't possibly make such a big decision in so short a time!'" But she did.

Looking back, Annette sees the events of her life as preparation for marrying Abner. In earlier years she had put her whole self into nursing and loved it, but when RNs became "paper nurses" and then "computer nurses," and when the work load increased as the staff was reduced, she lost interest in nursing. Burned out, stressed out, and pulled in too many directions, she quit working at the hospital after 28½ years. After a trip west with friends during five months of recovery, she took a job in home health services, and then a job supervising nurses in a health care unit. Now she sees this as preparation for marrying an older man and feeling comfortable with his age group.

Eventually, changes in working conditions took Annette to a different kind of work, and she stayed in that until three weeks before her wedding. She had planned to work part-time after marriage, but a bad situation at work made her decide to quit. This gave her the needed time to prepare for the wedding, and after marrying she did not need to work and could focus on their relationship. It was all in God's perfect timing.

While dating, Annette came across this verse,

". . . the Lord has done this, and it is marvelous in our eyes" (Psalm 118:23).

As for the future, Annette says, "We are on a waiting list for an apartment in a retirement community. Abner is ready to sell his things and go, but I am not ready yet to sell my things. I'm trying to adjust my thinking and trying to remember that he is 18 years older than I am."

A similar situation presents itself to another woman whose husband is 12 years older than she is. "This is the first time in 18 years," she says, "that our age difference has posed a challenge. My husband wants to sell our home and go to a retirement community. I am not ready for that. So we are praying about this and know that God will lead us where he wants us to be."

* * *

Apparently, one's age and one's energy level are not necessarily parallel. One woman whose husband is two and a half years older than she says, "He is active and in good health. He probably has more energy than I do."

Another says, "Even though he is seven years older than I, we were young and energetic at the time we married and didn't think about an age difference."

Still another says, "My husband is eight and a half years older than I, but his energy level is the same as mine or above. At 71 he is working harder than when we first married. He manages two farms for his sons. Sometimes the stress of it gets to him, but he is not one to sit around, and I guess all the activity keeps him young."

For Bertha, it was not so much a difference in energy levels, but the fact that she moved more slowly, even though she and her husband were the same age. She says, "With effort I learned to be on time, which is important to my husband."

Another woman, who is only two years younger than her husband, says she doesn't think it was age or necessarily energy level, "but he wanted to go to each and every meeting, and I would have been glad to stay at home more often."

"Even though my husband is nine years older," reports another wife, "he is well and has lots of energy. In walking he can outdo me. He is patient and walks with me."

Edna, who at age 69 married a man 80 years old, says his age was his worst feature, but she didn't find it too hard to accept. Furthermore, she says, "His energy level was okay as I never excelled in energy."

❉ ❉ ❉

Health problems can cause difficulties at any age in a marriage, no matter what the difference in ages. Most of the women who responded to my questions have handled aging and health problems well.

Elaine says that at the beginning of their marriage she and her husband both had high energy levels, "but as we are getting older, we notice differences, especially as declining health affects his energy level." Her husband is still involved in his business and in church work. As Elaine sees it though, it is not only one's energy level, but *how* each one functions. "When he gets tired," she says, "and his body tells him it is time to quit, he can leave whatever he is working on and go back to it at a later time. On the other hand, when I am doing a project, I will push to the completion of a job if at all possible, and then work with my body for having overdone it. I need to learn that it is okay if jobs take longer. When you're retired, you don't automatically slow down. But you do learn to live at a pace compatible with your energy, while at the same time trying to keep up your physical strength and endurance, as well as stretching your mind."

One woman, whose first husband was 10 years older than she, found that age was not a problem. "We did almost everything together," she says. "He was used to helping me." With her second husband it is different. He believes certain work is women's work. She can handle this because it is the mentality with which she was brought up. "He does dishes sometimes," she says, "and would help more in the house, yard, and garden, but his arthritis hinders him." When they go places together, she has to remember to slow down. "We can't travel just anywhere," she says. "But then we do other interesting things together."

Even though her husband is in the health care unit in a retirement home, a second wife who at age 64 married a man who was 80 says, "Having companionship again after 12 years as a widow was worth it all. He was a young 80, and we had 10 years of a wonderful marriage, sex included." Now she enjoys daily visits with him. "My greatest disappointment was that we didn't travel more together. He refused to fly, and I did most of the driving. He gave up driving at age 89, willingly, at my suggestion."

A 10 years' difference in age didn't create serious problems for one couple, until his diabetes caused him to be in a wheelchair. "Being younger," the second wife says, "I was able with the help of the children to take care of him at home for a while." So a younger wife benefited an older husband, and she didn't seem to mind being his caregiver.

After 17 years of marriage, Joanne needs to cope with the problem of her husband's hearing loss. Because his hearing loss makes it difficult for him to hear in church or in meetings, he now encourages her to go alone, which she often does.

Jewel also finds hearing loss to be a problem. She says it creates their biggest conflict. "I think he has heard what I said," she says, "but too often discover later that he didn't. I haven't solved this one, but I'm working on talking louder and plainer!"

Gathered Wisdom

1. Expect negative comments if you marry a person a lot older than you are. People may talk.
2. Be aware that your spouse may eventually need your care. Know that even if you are the same age, either one of you can become ill.
3. It is not age, as much as it is health, lifestyle, and good communication, that make for compatibility.
4. A hearing aid can improve one's quality of life. Anyone with a hearing loss would do well to make such an investment, even though a good one is costly.
5. Prepare for your husband's death, especially if he is a lot older than you are. Be able to be independent. Know how to keep the financial accounts, pay the bills, and balance the checkbook. Know about your car's upkeep. Be sure both of your wills are up-to-date and make sure that you understand them. Know what kind of funeral or memorial service and burial he wants. Also, know what his wishes are regarding advance medical directives; in other words, see that he has signed a living will and power of attorney.

MARCIA'S STORY

Bruce asked Marcia to sing in a trio at his wife's funeral. She didn't know if she could, because she felt that the Lord was saying that she would be in that home some day. But she sang. Bruce was a farmer with nine young children who needed a mother. Marcia was single, age 27, and had grown up on a farm with lots of younger siblings. Half a year later she got a letter from Bruce. She prayed and pondered for about six weeks, then wrote, making excuses about being too busy, but didn't give him an absolute no.

Soon he called her, and on their first date he told her that people gave him suggestions of women he might marry. He had 30 names. "I put the names all in a basket," he told Marcia, "and then knelt down to pray. I prayed that I'd pull out the name of one I should contact. And I pulled out your name."

Then Marcia told him of her struggle and how she knew she would be the one. So then and there, on their first date, they became engaged, and got married six weeks later.

"I think other people worried more than I did," she says, "about me marrying this widower."

They enjoyed 23 good years before he died of a heart attack on his 61st birthday. In addition to the original nine, they had three children together. The youngest was 19 when Marcia became a widow.

Marcia says, "When a man marries the second time, he will be so glad he has a wife, he will likely be good to you—gentle, kind, and considerate."

11.
BEING COMPARED WITH THE FIRST WIFE

Omar and I talk about Lois in connection with events in his past life, but I don't feel that he compares me with her in any way that has a negative effect on me. I don't recall that he has ever called me by her name, but friends who knew Omar and Lois have sometimes called me Lois. I did not know Lois personally, and I think that is probably an advantage. I appreciate the way I am accepted by Lois' family. Her mother once even referred to me as her daughter-in-law. I am the richer for being a part of three families.

✳   ✳   ✳

It seems that second wives who knew the first wife consider it an advantage, and some who did not know their husband's first wife feel it might have been helpful to have known her.

A friend told me this story about making comparisons. "I

never put water in the bottom of the pan when I roast a turkey. It draws its own juice. But my husband's family always put water in the pan. Once or twice my husband said, 'My wife did it this way.' That hurt, but it didn't happen often. And recently after he said, 'My wife . . . ' (I forget what it was about), he apologized."

"On the other hand," my friend told me, "his first wife had too many projects on the go; if she got tired of one, she started another. I found loads of partly finished needlework projects in the house. My husband doesn't like two or three things sitting around. When I start something he likes me to finish it, and I usually do, so in this way the comparison is favorable for me."

She knew his first wife well and had often heard her play the piano. "I don't play," she says. "I know he misses that and I feel sorry for him."

✻ ✻ ✻

Another said she felt good about having known the first wife. "If I hadn't known her," she says, "I think I'd always be curious about what type of person she was. My husband doesn't compare me with her. He says, 'That was then—this is now.'"

✻ ✻ ✻

Another second wife said she thought that not knowing the first wife was a disadvantage. She said, "I asked the children what their mother would have done in some situations, but they couldn't say. My husband does compare me with his first wife. A friend told me, 'A person who died will be glorified.' That helped me to overcome negative feelings about it."

✻ ✻ ✻

"I considered his first wife a friend," another wife says. "I feel it was an advantage to have known her because I can better understand his struggles with her long illness. We continue to get together with her siblings and I feel welcome with them. My husband is also welcomed by my first husband's family."

* * *

Another wife said, "Maybe once or twice the name slipped, and it didn't bother me in the least. He is very good about not comparing us. I know that I don't come up to her in cooking and so on. I did not know her and in some ways feel this is an advantage."

* * *

Another says, "I sometimes ask my husband what his first wife would have thought or done in a certain situation. He says I am like his first wife in many ways."

* * *

"The first wife was not a threat to me," says one woman, "because my husband never made me feel like a second wife. Only about twice did he call me by her name, and that wasn't a problem for me. I knew she was considered a wonderful person, and I wondered before our marriage how I could be an adequate wife for one who had such a wonderful first wife. But he made me feel by word and deed that I was special to him and loved. I think the husband has so much to do with how the second wife feels about his first wife. A while after we were married, I hoped that my husband wouldn't die before we had been married, as long as he and his first wife had been. If he had, it would have felt as if he had belonged to her more than to me."

* * *

Another friend told me, "I knew my husband's first wife well. He compared us by saying, 'The Lord gave me two good wives.' My second husband does sometimes compare us, but without meaning to hurt me."

"While I have never felt threatened by his first wife," says another woman, "at times I've thought I was not as brilliant as she was, nor as beautiful. But my husband has always assured me that I have qualities she didn't have and vice versa. I didn't try to be like her; I had only met her once very briefly."

One who married her brother-in-law said, "We talk about his first wife a lot; she was my sister. It's no problem."

"Not having known his first wife," said another second wife, "I really don't try to compare myself with her. I determined from the beginning I was going to be my own person."

* * *

Another second wife thinks the adjustment was hard for her husband. "After all," she says, "he was used to a woman doing things a certain way for many years. And with us, it was not only a difference in two women, it was also the cultural differences between our two countries, and the differences between a farm/homemaker woman and a career woman. His first wife was a wonderful cook, and I, having lived alone, often ate out. I had a lot to learn about cooking. I *did* know how to make pig stomach, but that wasn't a dish he was eager to explore! I've heard she was quite the pie-baker, and that's definitely not my gift. But I do make chocolate chip cookies to die for, and whoopie pies. The grandchildren are always asking for whoopie pies when they come. I'm not sure why I ever started making them because I can never keep enough on hand! And they take soooooo long to make!"

* * *

"Even though I did not know his first wife personally," says another second wife, "I heard enough about her giftedness that I tend to make comparisons. I find myself feeling inferior to her because I'm not able to be the grandmother she would have been. I feel that I lack the motherly instincts that come in a natural way to grandparents who have birthed and raised children. My husband does not and has not compared the two of us. He will talk about her and how she may or may not have done something, but it is never in a comparing way. Often his comments are about the way she worked with the children, and this is no problem to me."

* * *

"I never met her," said another wife, "but I have heard so many wonderful things about her from others that I am looking forward to meeting her in heaven. My husband and I find it comfortable talking to each other about our former companions, but I never feel that he is comparing me with her."

* * *

Another second wife says, "I knew his first wife casually, and felt inferior, but not to the point of it being a problem. She was 'his right arm' so to speak—a hard worker. My doctor told me I am more feminine than my husband's first wife was. She worked outdoors at his side, could do everything he did, and was a good manager. I suppose he's compared me with her, but he's never told me."

✳ ✳ ✳

"I worked with his first wife in a local bakery," reports another. "She was a loyal friend. She became sick and quit work about eight months before she died of lung cancer. Little did I know that three weeks later I would face the death of my husband. He died in his sleep of an apparent heart attack 11 days before his 70th birthday. So after one year, my bakery friend's husband came to visit me and asked permission to come some more. I consented to marry after much prayer and consideration. I know I was never able to replace her, but God is so good, and we can grow older together in the Lord."

✳ ✳ ✳

"My husband seldom mentioned her," says another wife, "and I do not think he compared me to her. My husband speaks of me as his very kind wife who has done much for him."

✳ ✳ ✳

"His first wife was my good friend," says another. "We grew up in the same church and school, and also graduated together. I was a gift receiver at their wedding. Our paths didn't cross often during their years together. He never compared me to her. Someone said I was a lot like her, and that that is why I fit into the family so well."

✳ ✳ ✳

"Does a parent love one child more than another? No," says one second wife. "In a second marriage, does one love one's new spouse better? No. Does one talk about the first spouse much? No. You are now in a new relationship. Neither of my two husbands expected me to be like his first spouse. I want my husband to love me for who I am, and I love him for who he is. It is a new beginning."

* * *

Another opinion is, "I believe you should always keep in memory your former spouses and not be afraid to mention their names as long as you don't compare your present spouse with a past one. No, my husband did not compare me with his first wife."

* * *

One who knew her husband and his first wife well from being together on the mission field, says, "As a nurse and friend, I helped when she was ill and was with her when she died. We are different. I am quiet; she was talkative." This second wife asked her husband if he minded that she was quiet and if she came up to his expectations. His answer was, "I chose you and I'm not disappointed." That satisfied her.

* * *

"I didn't want to be like his first wife," said another. "I just wanted to be myself! My husband compared us at first, and it didn't bother me, because he was only complimentary! He says I'm more like his mother!"

* * *

A widow who married a widower relates, "I was cutting corn off the cob with a knife. My husband said his first wife used a board and wondered why I didn't get one. But I liked to do it my way. I said, 'Well you don't do everything like my first husband, either.' But I never had a feeling that one of my husbands was better or worse than the other."

✳   ✳   ✳

One second wife says her husband talks more about his mother's cooking, or his grandma's, than his first wife's. She says, "We keep in touch with his first wife's family, and I enjoy going to their reunions."

✳   ✳   ✳

"During our first year together," reports another second wife, "my husband was still grieving. Having known his first wife, I could grieve with him as we talked and shared stories about the past. Instead of feeling threatened by it, I was moved by the loyalty and compassion he had, and I knew that would be there for me. I remembered his first wife as a good cook, and in that area I felt inferior. That was an adjustment for me."

✳   ✳   ✳

Another wife says she thinks she and her second husband might say, "This is the way we did it in the past, but how are we going to do it now?" She reflects that conflict can sometimes occur because "this isn't how I'm used to doing something." On such occasions, she and her husband might compare their pasts and their present, but they never do it in a way that puts the other one down.

CATHY'S STORY

When Cathy graduated from nurses' training, the employment she thought she had lined up disappeared, so she finished school without a job in view.

Some weeks later she received two letters—one from the hospital where she graduated, asking her to come in for an interview; the other a letter from a mission board asking her to consider going to Ethiopia. She dismissed the latter and set up an appointment to interview for the hospital job.

Cathy thought, Surely God wouldn't ask me to go to Ethiopia at my age and as a single. *She didn't want to give up her hopes for a husband and family. But God didn't let her off the hook that easily. He and she had a battle one day when God seemed to be directing her to go to Ethiopia, and she felt that God couldn't ask that of her. Eventually, she agreed to go, and God gave her peace of mind about going.*

The day Cathy left New York by ship, a young missionary wife died on the mission field in Ethiopia. After the month-long trip to Ethiopia, she learned to know the young widowed husband during six weeks of language study in the city where he served. Several months after she left for her assignment about 300 miles away, she received a letter from the young widower. Postal service wasn't very good, but they did manage to get letters to

*each other, and she occasionally got to the city on vaca-
tion. Their friendship developed into a lasting relationship. Cathy says, "Apparently God was only testing me to
see if I was willing to give up a family for him!" In time
God gave her a husband and family, too.*

12.
PERSONALITY TRAITS, LIKES, AND DISLIKES

Knowing that Omar and I both like to talk, one of our friends wondered which of us would do the listening. I hadn't thought of that as a problem, but sometimes I have gotten tired standing after a meeting while Omar tells long stories which I've already heard, but which others seem to enjoy hearing.

On the other hand, I soon learned that Omar liked a lot of quiet time. In bed at night I'd be chattering away and getting little response from him. He was too tired to talk. I said, "I get tired, but never too tired to talk." So I learned to be quiet, and later found that even I can get too tired to talk. We both feel comfortable with long stretches of silence while sitting together reading, while traveling, and while working or eating. But we still find time for good open communication with each other. We both enjoy talking *and* listening *and* being quiet.

One of our biggest "likes and dislikes" problems centered around an afghan. A few months into our marriage, I picked up the yellow, orange, and brown afghan his 22-year-old daughter, who was now my daughter, too, had made. "Look, Omar. You probably don't like this one either if you don't like mine with the gold, coral, and pink stripes," I challenged him.

"Well," he hesitated, "I do prefer the color combination on the one Rachel made."

Our daughter, knowing her father's narrow tastes, cheered at hearing that her father liked something she had made. But I reacted, "How dare you!"

Determined not to be outdone, I pulled my afghan from the closet, proceeded in a grandiose way to spread it on the living room sofa, and playfully praised its elegance. All three of us laughed . . . as I turned away to hide my tears.

Later that evening, alone with my husband, I could control my tears no longer. "I was really upset about that afghan even though I laughed."

"I thought so," he said. "I know you put a lot of work into it, and it is beautifully done. I like the design—especially the gold stripes in popcorn stitch. It's those pink stripes . . . ."

"But I made it just like the pattern in the book!"

"However, not everyone needs to like the pattern. It's a matter of personal taste."

So here it was again, this matter of his narrow personal tastes. He has excellent tastes, but I like a wider range of things. When we choose things together we can eventually find something that we both like. But I had made this afghan *before* our recent marriage.

When he first saw it and I told him I had made it, he didn't say much. Only later did I realize that those pink stripes really distressed him.

As a compromise, we planned a pattern and chose the colors together for an afghan that we would *both* like. Joyfully I started to crochet *our* afghan.

Meanwhile, I draped the one with the pink stripes over a chair in our guest room. Then I stashed it away in the closet for a while. One day I decided, *I'll sell this afghan. I'd be better off having the money.*

The gift buyer held it up and admired it, then paused and said, "But the pink stripes . . ." Omar and I eyed each other knowingly and could hardly keep a straight face. It was beginning to be funny.

Months later I picked up my *unsold* afghan from the gift shop. Again I draped it over the chair, folding it so the pink parts didn't show.

Then we could talk about it with less emotion. My hurt diminished as our love grew stronger. It had become sort of a symbol for us about little differences in marriages. We could look at each other knowingly and say, "Pink stripes in the afghan!"

Another slight difference for us is the matter of clutter. Omar and I both like a clutter-free house, but I sometimes find him a little extreme. If I set the jars by the basement door to be taken down later, he might ask where they are going. Then he'll make a special trip to the basement with them. We have kept such a clutter-free house that sometimes it has been difficult for us to agree on when it needs to be cleaned. He thinks that if things are in order, cleaning is not so necessary. I think we need to dust and vacuum once in a while. But we have worked this one out quite well. After we were both retired, I didn't feel that the house must be cleaned each week. When we do clean, he graciously does the vacuuming for me. We have also hired someone to clean occasionally. The clutter has to go somewhere, and for us that is into drawers and closets. Omar has been more of a pack rat than I have been. He has boxes and boxes of old letters, scads of cassette tapes, photos albums, and slides. Now we're thinking about downsizing and working together at what to keep and what to get rid of.

Thelma found that Mark doesn't like clutter either. She had a Cat's Meow and an angels collection, but she hasn't bought any new figures since she's married. Mark doesn't like those kinds of things sitting around. This is not a problem for Thelma.

Thelma and Mark have their love for travel in common, but while Thelma would like to go back to see a certain place again, Mark says, "After we've seen everything else." He wants to see new things.

It's not always the man who dislikes clutter. The thing that upsets one wife the most is her husband's accumulation of antiques and old things. "I can hardly stand it," she says. "I like things neat and orderly, and he packs and stacks. It took days to get ready for sale on his farm. And his house was full when I came into it. We did a lot of clearing out, and I thought we had things under control, but as his daughters say, 'That's him.'"

This issue comes between them more than anything else. He gets upset if she fusses about it, and yet she can hardly stand the clutter in their garage and cellar. "And I have to keep after him in the house to see that it doesn't accumulate there," she says. "He just can't get rid of things—papers and mail and stuff. If I nag him all the time, it just causes friction. So I have to learn to live with it, but it's difficult. It's caused a lot of stress in my life. I think he should give in and be more considerate, and he thinks I should just let him be. I told him I don't know any woman who would have put up with this any more agreeably than I have."

* * *

Eunice says her husband liked antiques and she did not. He said he lost some interest in antiques after his first wife died. "But recently that interest is coming back. I can accept his going to sales," Eunice says, "because it gives me space. Since retirement we are together a lot."

* * *

One second wife told me, "When we have conflicts in our marriage, it's about our differences." She and her husband have found a lot of common ground, but she thinks their different backgrounds caused some adjustment problems. She is more reserved, and he hugs everybody and rubs women's shoulders. She feels like, "Whoa! Wait a minute! That's a little borderline!"

Another difficulty between them is travel. She likes to go to the mountains in the snow, and he hates the cold. He likes to go to a Christian music festival and sit out in the sun when it's 95 degrees. She hates the heat. But they do what they each dislike for the other. "We'll go to the cabin in the snow in January or February, and we'll go to 'Creation' in the summer with all the children." She says, "Also I hate crowds and the glitzy stuff, and he tends to be a people person and doesn't mind mobs." (He says, "Not exactly, but I tolerate them.")

This same wife says that communication is the biggest key—being able to say, "That hurt me when you did that," as opposed to keeping quiet about it. One of the strong points of their marriage is that they can both be fairly open. They talk a lot, besides having God foremost.

* * *

Joyce and her husband both like to travel, but she gets tired of living out of a suitcase.

"He gets up early," Joyce says, "and I get up a little later, and he doesn't nag me about it. He's flexible, but I think it might bug him if I stayed in bed too long."

❋ ❋ ❋

Amanda's husband likes to attend a lot of meetings. She likes to go, too, but wishes they'd stay home sometimes. She says, "I'd rather not go quite so much, but I go with him. He will give in sometimes if I say I don't think we'd have to go this time. We compromise between doing it his way and my way."

Amanda likes to read, and since she's married she doesn't have a chance to read as much as she did before. But she wouldn't exchange her married life for being single. She thoroughly enjoys the companionship.

❋ ❋ ❋

Jewel is glad that her husband accepts her friends as his own. She had lots of friends, both married and single, and she loves to hear him talk about them as "our friends." She says, "I've known of some second marriages where the husband couldn't care less about learning to know his wife's friends. My husband and I have really learned to enjoy each other's friends. We have many good times with his friends, too."

❋ ❋ ❋

"We both like to walk, cycle, travel, and listen to music," says Stella. But she wants quiet when she needs to concentrate. He likes TV more than she does, and he also reads more than she does. Details are important to her. Their values are similar, and they both enjoy giving. They balance each other. He says he learned more from her about being thoughtful, like stopping to help someone with trouble along the highway.

＊ ＊ ＊

Fran had a pleasant surprise when she learned that her husband, as she did, had the habit of going to sleep with the radio on.

＊ ＊ ＊

Bertha says she tends to move slowly, and that being prompt is very important to Dan. "He didn't scold me," she says, "but I knew it was a major issue for him to be on time. I worked hard and feel that I have conquered that one. I seldom make him wait anymore."

＊ ＊ ＊

Pat's first husband would buy cases of food when it was on special, and he kept gallons of water and lots of extra things on hand. Her present husband is quite the opposite. "I like to have basics on hand and not run to the store so often," she says, "but he doesn't see that it's necessary to buy on ahead. He'd rather just go to the store and get it when we need it."

Her husband had a little fun with this difference at Christmas. "We had agreed not to buy each other gifts," Pat said. "Then on Christmas morning here he came with a gift beautifully wrapped for me. I said, 'I'm not opening this. We had agreed not to get each other gifts.' But he insisted I open it. Guess what! It was a gallon of 'bought' water. Well, this gave us a good laugh. This was the Christmas before the much-talked-about Y2K turn-of-the-century, and I had thought we should have water on hand. He didn't think that was necessary."

Pat also mentioned several other little differences. "He gets up early and doesn't seem to need as much sleep as I do, but he doesn't object to my sleeping later in the morning. He is sensitive to my wishes."

＊ ＊ ＊

Marcia and Elva both married men who like to go hunting, and they both accepted it well. Marcia likes music and her husband wasn't much of a singer, but they had many other interests in common, such as travel and snowmobiling.

✳ ✳ ✳

A nurse, who married a farmer, is conscious of germs spreading infection, while he seems to think it laborious to wash his hands as often as she would like. She also misses having time to herself. Since he is retired, he is around most of the time. She sometimes likes to go out to eat with her friends without him. This bothered him at first, but he later agreed that she should keep contact with her friends and relatives. She knows so many people, and when they go somewhere and she meets and talks with friends, he is bored and annoyed. But she still says he was worth waiting for and these differences do not spoil her happy marriage.

✳ ✳ ✳

Amy says, "As we become older we are more set in our ways, but we can work it out." Her husband didn't like to have bright lights on. And he wanted to go to church whenever anything was happening there. She enjoyed going but didn't think they *always* had to be there. They both enjoy visiting. "It was a great part of his life," she says, "to visit families experiencing conflict. His being there seemed to be valuable—giving people opportunity to talk. He could quote Scripture, and I enjoyed this, too."

✳ ✳ ✳

Susan is amazed at how much her second husband is like her first husband—gentle and soft-spoken. She says, "We like the same music and food, and I had no adjustments in cooking. He compliments me almost every meal."

Janette reflects about her deceased second husband, "We both liked to travel, and we both liked to read, but different types of reading. We both walked. One difference was that he took everything so calmly. I felt like, 'Why don't you react?' But then his calmness helped us through difficulties. I had to learn to be more flexible. I had always dreamed of traveling and thought it would never be realized, but in my second marriage it happened. To my delight we traveled to Europe twice, and to other places."

✳ ✳ ✳

Gathered Wisdom

1. Keep your mind open to the differences between you and your spouse. Look for the good.
2. You may think, "If only my first husband were still living." You have to face the fact that your first marriage is over.
3. Find out before marriage what your prospective husband thinks about money, cars, giving, music, antiques, clutter in the house, and so on. You can live with differences more easily if you understand and accept each other's likes and dislikes.
4. Know what his expectations of you are before you marry. Be sure that he doesn't expect you to be a different person than you are. Be sure he will let you be yourself.
5. If you are going to remarry, do not count on your second marriage being the same as your first marriage. You'd better be flexible. And if you always want to have things your way, don't remarry.
6. Don't rush into a second marriage. Take long enough to get to know each other. Discuss your likes and dislikes, your beliefs, convictions, and values.
7. One second wife advises, "After the death of a spouse, go through a year of all the difficult days—birthdays, anniversaries, and holidays—before becoming involved in another serious relationship." But others believe you can start a relationship before a year has passed, and that some of the grieving can be done even after remarrying. A good second marriage can help to relieve the loneliness and grief.

JULIA'S STORY

Julia says, "I had no idea that Wilbur was interested in me. I was at his first wife's funeral, and a thought came to my mind—he's a widower and I could be his wife. But I quickly threw that in the back of my mind. I didn't even want to think about marrying a widower. I thought of Wilbur as a pioneer who could carry out a ministry on his own. I admired his stability and prayerful attitude."

About eight months later, Julia went to a singles retreat where Wilbur was one of the speakers. Only much later did she learn of the struggles he was going through at that time. He had just come back from an overseas trip and drove to the retreat all by himself. Experiencing homesickness and grief, he prayed on the way that God would give him another life companion, and he secretly hoped that Julia would be there. (If she would have known!) After arriving at the camp and finding his assigned room, he was scheduled to attend a prayer meeting with the other speakers. When he opened the door and stepped into the hall, the first person he saw was Julia. He told her he had just been in Belize, and she replied, "Oh, we'll have to talk some more."

"Very innocent!" she says. "We did talk a little more that weekend (enough to give Wilbur a new spark in his heart). Later, I was a little haunted by how Wilbur's eyes looked when we met. He acted kind of nervous or shy. I noticed, but I gave it no thought. Later it all made sense."

About four months later Wilbur contacted Julia's father while she was at work, asking him about Julia. Wilbur asked her dad to pray about it and said that he may tell Julia about his phone call if he wanted to. The day Wilbur called, Julia and her dad had been car shopping, and the next day she wanted to show her mother the car she was interested in. Her dad suddenly said, "Well, Julia, maybe you don't need a car!"

"Why?" she asked.

"Last evening a man called."

Julia quickly burst out with, "Was it a widower or a single man?"

He said, "A widower."

Her heart sank.

Her parents asked her to guess, and she remembers, "It just popped into my mind—Wilbur, from Pennsylvania. What made me think of him? I'm convinced the thought came from God. I realized then that God was bringing us together. But that was also the beginning of a troubled mind. I had to make peace with marrying a widower, which I had said I would never do. I had always thought a lot of Wilbur and admired his character. I really didn't feel worthy of him."

He didn't call back for a while, and Julia thought, He probably gave up on me after all. That was kind of a relief, and yet a letdown. She prayed that if this relationship wasn't God's will, that Wilbur wouldn't call back.

But he did call.

He called her dad again, and he said he'd write a letter. One weekend when she had some friends in, she had a feeling that a letter from him was in the mailbox. She thought, That letter is better off staying there till I get home from work Monday morning. *(She was on the midnight shift.) Then she enjoyed the weekend with her friends!*

As expected, the letter was in her mailbox Monday morning. She nervously opened the well written letter. "It did not play on my emotions or guilt," *she said.* "He was informative and factual. He said he'd call me in a couple of weeks to see how I was feeling, but that I didn't need to give him an answer then.*

"The confirmation I felt is something I can't explain. I had a real peace about accepting his friendship."

When he called, she was not as nervous as she expected to be, and she even enjoyed their talk. "I told him I felt honored that he thought of me!" *she says.* What a thing to tell a man! I didn't realize how it made his heart take a leap. *But she waited for a month to give him an answer. A few weeks later they spent an evening together for the first time. It wasn't long until they decided to marry.*

13.
SEXUAL
ADJUSTMENT

On the day of our wedding, a married friend told me, "Don't worry about what happens the first night. Just relax and enjoy giving to each other what you needed to hold back before marriage." I had done some reading in preparation and felt I was ready and not fearful. However, my friend's advice helped me relax when things did not go quite like the book that first night!

As time went on, I found being in bed with my husband to be a satisfying and sometimes hilarious experience. I marveled again and again at how God created us male and female. I believe I thought more about sex before marriage and during the first year than I did later. I didn't need to fantasize and dream when I had a husband and when my needs were satisfied. I think sex is played up in the media to be more important than it is. It is important, but I think companionship in marriage is even more significant.

* * *

Sex is such a personal matter that I didn't know if I should ask questions about it. But some of the women who answered my questions did want to talk about it.

* * *

A young couple who were both married before commented: "Sex is a gift when you adore your spouse, when you're working and that's who you're thinking about. Sex is a natural result of adoring that person, especially when that person accepts you for who you are. Sex brings us back together. It's not what our relationship is based on, but sex is great because our relationship is good."

* * *

"It all just came so naturally. No problems," one second wife who had been single into her 60s told me.

* * *

"We enjoy each other very much," offered another woman. She reflected that it's different than it would be if they were younger. She pointed out that the most important thing is not sex, but companionship. "Knowing I am loved unconditionally by my husband is such a secure feeling. He tells me and shows me he loves me and often puts me and my desires above his." She says her husband is all that she wanted and more.

* * *

One finds her second husband to be more affectionate than her first. Later he became impotent, and that, she says, bothers him more than it bothers her.

* * *

While many older couples make excellent adjustments, a number that I spoke with have had difficulty sexually, mostly due to problems connected with aging or illness. Many older men have problems with impotence. With advice from doctors or counselors, some have received help by using mechanical aids or medications, while others are satisfied with manual stimulation.

But even with these problems, as one says, "We have a lot of fun together."

Gathered Wisdom

1. Relax, and don't feel guilty if your sexual activity does not go like the books say it will or it should.
2. Live a wholesome, healthful lifestyle, and get enough exercise.
3. Don't expect to be as active as younger people, but try to have you and your partner be content with your intimate relationship.
4. If you feel you have serious problems, don't hesitate to get professional counseling.

MARIA'S STORY

Marie had dated her present husband for a short time before his first marriage. When his wife passed away, she sent him a sympathy card, but it never entered her mind that she would date him again. When he called her she declined to see him, saying she felt he had not waited long enough. This gave her time to think.

She began to feel that marrying might be God's will for her, so sometime later she wrote him a note saying that she would be willing to plan something with him. After one date, he invited her to a family picnic at his first wife's brother's home. His three young children came along with their grandparents. When it was time to eat, the children came in from playing. When his daughter came in, Marie said, "Well, this must be Melissa."

Marie continues her story, "Melissa ran to me, crawled up on my lap, and we looked at a book together. His son talked with me at the table. On the way home, Melissa sat between her father and me, laid her head on my lap, and soon fell fast asleep. I liked it.

"After dating 4½ months we were married. I can't remember having any fears about marrying and becoming an 'instant mother.' I knew God was leading, and he has continued to lead us, one day at a time. Many people prayed for us."

14.
BURIAL PLANS

One of the most difficult decisions I had to make soon after Omar and I were married concerned burial plans. Omar was in the process of buying a gravestone to place at his first wife, Lois,' grave. Of course, he wanted to have his name inscribed on it, too. He offered to put my name on it also and to provide space for me to be buried next to them. The cemetery is at Lois' home church, in an area not very familiar to me. This was an emotional struggle for me, but I decided, "Yes, I will be buried with Omar and Lois and have my name on the stone." It seemed the right thing to do.

✳ ✳ ✳

Nearly each one of the women who responded to this question, and who were single and married widowers, plans to be buried beside her husband and his first wife. And nearly each one of the widows who married widowers will be buried beside her first spouse.

Evelyn had a decision to make similar to mine. She says, "I was an only child, and my name had been put on the tombstone of my parents. When we got married, Frank had not yet bought a tombstone for his first wife. So we discussed this, and I had to make up my mind about whether I wanted to stay with my parents or be buried with my husband. I decided I wanted to be buried with my husband. So he got a tombstone that has all three names on it, and my name was removed from my parents' tombstone."

One woman has requested that her body be donated for medical science.

In a situation where the first wife died on the mission field, the man and his second wife will be buried together in the States.

One woman's first husband provided a burial lot for her in the state where his first wife was buried, but recently she sold it to a son. She married a second time, has more relatives now in her home state, and will likely be buried with her second husband.

Sylvia showed her sense of humor in her response. "I hope to have a cemetery marker next to Tony's with his first wife on the other side. Maybe he could be tipped a bit toward my side!"

One second wife finds this matter to be a problem because she would like to be buried with her husband, but there isn't room beside him and his first wife. There is room for her next to her parents, and their tombstone has a place for her name on it. At the time of my interview with her, she didn't know what she and her husband would decide.

Another woman already had her tombstone and will be buried where it is placed. Her husband will be buried with his first wife in another cemetery in the same community.

One couple has never discussed the matter. The husband has never indicated that he wants his second wife buried near him. He knows that she has a plot of her own which she had before their marriage.

Another husband has his burial plans made and funeral expenses taken out of his account. He had a small stone with his first wife's name on it. There would have been room for his second wife to be buried in his lot, but she refused, so he sold that to his son. She preferred to be buried in the lot of her parents,' where her name is already on the family stone. (She had earlier decided she was not going to be married.) There is a photo of the second wife with her husband on his tombstone, and a similar photo on her family stone, so in that way she is identified with him.

But one second wife has different feelings about whose names are where. Her husband has his name on his first wife's tombstone. She says, "To be honest, that hurt my feelings when I saw it, but he said he just didn't think of how it would be if he ever married again. But there is a burial place beside their plot for me. When I die what difference will it make?!"

Another says, "My husband's first wife is buried in our church cemetery, and my husband has a double tombstone with their names on it. Plans are for me to be buried beside his first wife. That's okay with me, but I don't like to look at the stone."

NORMA'S STORY

About four months after the death of Norma's husband, Norma was giving thanks to God for the way he was taking care of her. The Lord spoke to her about a widower who was going through a similar experience, and God's voice said that he was preparing the widower for her. It was a surprise to Norma, because marrying again was the least of her thoughts, but she told the Lord she would accept. She says, "When I met this man, I knew immediately that he was the one. In our 15 years of marriage we have never doubted God's leading."

15.
It Doesn't Always Work Out Well

When Pat told her single friend that she was getting married, her friend sighed and said, "These second marriages!"

"What about them?" Pat asked.

"You know some of them don't go very well. How old are you? Who is it, and how old is he?" she asked.

When Pat told her that they were ages 77 and 78, the friend said, "Well, if it doesn't go well, you won't have long to be miserable."

Pat replied, "But I expect it *will* go well." Pat's marriage is working out well, as are the marriages of most of the women I interviewed.

It is still true that some women do get into abusive situations in second marriages. I know a couple of women who had good first marriages, but who are no longer living with the widower they married.

When Anita and Tom married in their 50s, he treated her like a queen until they had their marriage license. Immediately he started making unreasonable demands—he wanted her to pay to take his children along on their honeymoon, which she refused to do.

Tom didn't allow Anita to bring any of her furniture or dishes to his house; she came only with a suitcase of clothes and a few personal things. He told her there was no closet space for her. He did all the grocery shopping, and she had to cook what he ordered.

After a few months Anita knew that she had made the biggest mistake of her life. The first Christmas was a disaster; he bought his children expensive items and very little for her children. Her children soon knew they were not welcome in Tom's home.

Anita went into a depression, and she went for counseling. Tom refused to go to counseling. He abused her spiritually, emotionally, and physically. On a Sunday morning after he had slapped her, the hymns in church made her cry. He said, "Can't you even behave in church for one hour?" At that point she got up and went out, drove home, got out the pills, and almost ended it all, but she thought of her children and couldn't do it.

The next week she told the counselor what she had almost done. The counselor called Tom and said, "I would like you to come along next time. I need to talk with you so I can better understand your wife's problem."

He agreed to go along and, to Anita's surprise, he actually did. The counselor soon saw Tom's contradicting personalities and, after he dismissed him, told Anita that Tom is a schizophrenic.

Anita said to Tom, "Before marriage you treated me like a queen. But as soon as the papers were signed you were different. Why?" But she got no satisfactory answer.

Anita prayed earnestly, and her answer seemed to be, "Go back to the farm. Your son needs you. You cannot take this any longer." So she decided to do that, having put up with the marriage for almost a year.

On the day she planned to leave, Tom kissed her goodbye before going to work, and she told him, "I don't know if I'll be here when you get back."

He said, "Whatever." And that's all he said.

She hugged his daughter and they cried together. She took her suitcase of clothes and her few personal belongings and went back to the farm where her children warmly welcomed her.

Two weeks later Anita went back to the counselor. He said, "You look so much better. Did something good happen?"

She told him what took place. He said he hadn't wanted to tell her to leave, but he didn't see how she stood it as long as she did. He advised her to have the marriage annulled. Her lawyer explained that if she didn't do this, Tom could buy anything and charge it to her. But the counselor said, "You must tell Tom. Tell him about the annulment."

When she called Tom and told him, she listened while he called her all sorts of horrible names. Then she asked, "Is there anything else you want to say?"

He said, "No."

The papers went through in a hurry. She told her counselor, "I felt like I had a ball and chain around my neck and now the shackles all fell off."

Another second wife put up with an abusive spouse for several years before moving out. Yet she does not say her marriage was a mistake. She was able to help his children by showing them a different way of life from what they had known.

Gathered Wisdom

1. Before marrying a widower, find out from his relatives and neighbors how he treated his first wife. Also, observe how he relates to others.

2. During courtship, arrange a picnic with his family. Notice how the children help or don't help with the preparations and cleanup, and how they relate to their father.

3. Before marriage, refuse to do something he suggests or wants to do and see how he reacts.

4. Watch out for signs of an abuser. It may not be easy to see these indicators during courtship, but try to be aware of any suspicious actions, words, or behavior.

5. Look for any one or more of the following signs:
   - Will not go for counseling, and/or forbids you to go.
   - Does not show affection.
   - Never gives compliments.
   - Never says "we" but always "I."
   - Makes threats to children such as, "If you don't do as I say I'll lock you in the trunk of my car." (Don't consider and overlook such remarks as being joking.)
   - Controls his family harshly.
   - Can be nice to people in public but is different at home.
   - Belittles wife and/or children, even in the presence of others.
   - Frequently changes churches, or starts his own church, or joins a cultic group.
   - Tries to isolate you from your friends and family; shows or expresses jealousy.

THELMA'S STORY

When Thelma heard that Mark's wife had passed away, she had a special feeling about Mark that she just couldn't explain. She knew Mark and his first wife well; they went to the same church. One evening she had Mark over for a meal, together with Chet, whom she had been dating. She thought, Well, we're friends, what's wrong with having two men for dinner?

Sometime later Mark called on the phone and said, "I just want to let you know that I think a lot of you."

Then she said something about not being committed to Chet. Reflecting back, Thelma says, "I sometimes think now that I pushed this along as much as he did."

She agreed to go out with Mark one evening, and he asked, "Do you mind going for a little drive?" He didn't want people he knew to see them right away, so they went to the next city to eat.

Then they didn't go out together for a while, and Thelma continued her friendship with Chet. She saw Chet as a good friend and someone to go away with, but he was not interested in getting married. Finally she told him, "I think it's time we break this off."

Then she called Mark and told him, "I'm free now."

When people at their church saw them together, several surprised them by making comments such as, "We're so happy about this; we prayed and prayed about this." They felt greatly affirmed that people thought they should be together.

16.
ONE HUSBAND'S EXPERIENCE: ROGER'S STORY

Roger met Rosene in a support group designed to meet the specific needs of widowed parents with young children. They had not known each other, nor each other's spouses. It was Rosene who invited Roger to join the group—not directly, but through a mutual friend. She had heard about Roger's wife's illness and death. Roger says, "We had no thought that this could lead to match-making."

Roger says that people grieve at different speeds. He also points out that when your spouse is terminal, and you know for an extended period of time that s/he will die (in his case, eight months), you start the grieving process then, even though you don't realize it. "You go into a survival mode," he says, "but deep down you're starting to separate yourself."

He went through intense periods of grieving until about four months after his wife died. By the time he joined the support group, he was past the really intense time, but he was trying to figure out if his reactions were normal. There he started hearing, "Oh, hey, that's normal. Other people do this, too." He can't encourage people enough to join a support group. It really helped him.

Roger started with the group in February, and it was in April that he began to really notice Rosene. "But I thought, 'Oh Roger, no! Her husband just died. Don't even think about it.'"

He told himself, "And besides, you've been away from dating so long you wouldn't even know how to ask anybody out anymore. And so, no, forget it."

But the Lord gave them a way to learn to know each other that was not threatening. Roger works with computers, and Rosene wanted another computer. So he set out to help her find one. "We got acquainted with each other very innocently through email," Roger said. "We emailed back and forth. I'd give her some advice about computers, and we kept that up for about six weeks, while still attending the support group. Then gradually, instead of discussing the best computer to get, we started sharing more personal questions. The first anniversary of my wife's death came along, and we asked each other how things were going, and we talked about our children."

Then the support group decided to go out to eat together, and Roger had a coupon which he shared with Rosene. She didn't know where the restaurant was, so they met outside of town and she followed him in. "She was concerned about whether this was okay with me," Roger says, "because it was a restaurant where my first wife and I had gone to eat several times."

Roger insists that God pushed him into asking Rosene for a dating relationship. He says, "The whole time I'm feeling this urge but telling God, 'You don't know what you're talking about. You know, six months since her husband died. There's no way, . . . God, I know better here."

During the meal he didn't trust to look at Rosene lest he give something away or say something stupid. He kept chatting away with the woman on the other side of him. He says, "Rosene told me later, she thought, 'Oh wow! Isn't that something? I believe he must be interested in her.'"

"After the meal," Roger continues, "I had a computer book to give to Rosene, and I was scared to death. I felt God was pushing me to ask her, but I fought him kicking and screaming. I never experienced anything like this before. It was so real, the prompting of the Holy Spirit, God saying to me, 'Yes, do it.' I can't explain it."

Rosene asked him, "Are you okay? Are you dealing with this okay?" She was still thinking about the fact that he had eaten in this same restaurant with his first wife.

He said, "No, I'm struggling, but it's got nothing to do with that."

She said, "Well, then, what are you struggling with?"

He says he just blurted out, "Well, I'm not sure how I should ask you out."

"I was scared to death," he says. "And all she said was three words. She looked at me and said, 'Just hold me.' So I hugged her. That was the beginning of our dating. Rosene told me later that there was something extremely comforting in that hug. It felt right to her. But she doesn't advise people to base their future relationships only on that kind of gesture."

Roger says their way of sensing their future is not something you would advise in a manual, but it is a "How God Led" kind of story.

They started seeing each other, and Roger says so many things began falling into place that he felt confident God was directing them. "I'd been praying about it," he says, "because I always felt God had helped me pick my first wife, and so I said, 'Okay, God, I want you to help me pick my second wife.'

"But Rosene really struggled about it," he says. "She didn't feel as certain as I did. One time she went to her sister's house for three days to be totally alone and do nothing but seek God's direction. She resisted the temptation to watch TV, because she didn't want some romantic love story to make her think, 'Oh, yeah, I want to get married again.' She wanted to hear God's voice. She says she really looked for a miraculous answer, like a dream in which her deceased husband would come to her and say, 'Go ahead,' or that she would hear a definite yes or no from God. She was ready to say, 'I don't want this marriage if this isn't what you want.' But God didn't give her a miraculous answer, and she was terrified, especially for her children."

On top of that, Roger and Rosene both coped with conflicting advice from friends. Some thought their romance was happening too soon. Roger says, "And I'm not saying that is bad advice. If one of our daughters were to go through a similar circumstance, I'd probably say exactly the same thing. But I felt God had brought us together."

Roger received an encouraging word from a friend around the time he and Rosene became engaged. After he told his friend about dating Rosene, the friend told him something that happened a few months earlier. He had awakened from a dream, looked at his wife, and said, "You wouldn't believe the dream I had. I dreamed that Roger is marrying this woman, who is my sister's neighbor." And Rosene was his sister's neighbor. God had spoken to a man Roger highly trusted. At that point Roger said, "Okay, God." Up to that point he knew, but there were children involved, and a lot of complications. Only then did he know for sure.

Then came the problem of where to live. They each owned a house, but they soon realized that not just any house could accommodate this new family with seven children—his three, ages 13, 14, and 16, and her four, ages seven, 10, 12, and 15. Her house was too small and his was in a school district they didn't want to be in. They thought of enlarging her house. Finding no easy way to do it, they thought about building a new home, but their search for a lot on which to build turned up nothing.

"And then," Roger says, "while surfing the Internet, I stumbled across a house in a quiet neighborhood with a fair-sized lot." They looked at the outside and saw how rundown it was. Skeptical, they mulled over the idea and one morning took the children to see it.

They prayed, "God, if you want this to be the house, we want some sign." And they agreed that if any of the children, even one, had any objection, they would take that as a no. Some had hesitancies about moving, but not one of them said they didn't like the house.

So they bought the place, and then all pitched in and remodeled the big house. Everyone contributed to the house's new condition, and there they made a fresh start as a new family. They all felt it was the right thing to have done. Roger thinks he would not have minded living in the house where Rosene had lived with her first husband. But he knows Rosene was thankful they didn't choose one of their previous houses because of vivid memories of having lived there with their former spouses.

Of course there were adjustments. But Roger says, "We have found common ground. When you lose a spouse you lose your dreams with the spouse; you don't realize it, but you bury the dreams at the same time." But now he and

Rosene are building new dreams. "We have a dream already, that when the children reach a certain age, this house is going to be way too big for the two of us! So we're going to build a log cabin. We have dreams of vacations, too, and plans for trips."

Fran's Story

A young man who worked with Fran asked her, "Would you be interested in meeting my father? He is so lonely." He invited Fran to his house for dinner, along with his father, and it was as if they had known each other all of their lives.

Fran recalls that when she had read his first wife's obituary in the paper (and she had never met either of them), it seemed like something said to her, "You're going to marry that man."

He started taking her out to eat, and she invited him to her house for dinner. They met in March and got married in December. Her life's guiding verse is:

"Have I not commanded you? Be strong and courageous. Do not be terrified; do not be discouraged, for the Lord your God will be with you wherever you go" (Joshua 1:9).

17.
ANOTHER HUSBAND'S EXPERIENCE: LAMAR'S STORY

At the suggestion of a friend, LaMar scheduled a week at a camp after his wife died. "Alone, yet with people nearby," he says, "I had time to grieve and sort out my thoughts without the pressure of daily schedules at home." The retreat also gave him time to go through the many cards and letters he had received.

"I thought about remarriage very soon after LuAnn's death—too soon to admit at the time," LaMar says. He thinks this was partly because he was lonely, but also, he says, "Because our marriage was so good, I wanted another good relationship. I also knew that my dreams either had to be abandoned or to be re-born in another relationship." LaMar feared losing too much of life if none of his dreams could be realized, and he was eager to try to fulfill them. "But I needed time to rethink my lifestyle, what to do about the house we owned, and what my children (who were all grown) needed and were going through."

Early on, LaMar was attracted to Lynn, but he tried to put it aside. He knew of her very recent bout with cancer, but he didn't know what the prognosis was or whom to ask about it. He confided in his counselor about his interest in Lynn and his reluctance to marry someone who might suffer a return of cancer. "His response was golden," reflects LaMar. The counselor asked, "Do you have a guarantee that you'll be here in five years?"

Meanwhile, LaMar made a list of about 20 qualities he felt he needed or wanted in his future wife. After he and Lynn had been dating for a short while, he checked the list. He says, "I found she met or exceeded almost every quality on the list!"

"When we started dating," LaMar recalls, "whenever we were driving somewhere together, we would both be so interested in what the other was saying, that we would end up making a wrong turn or getting lost. And it's still happening!"

Just before asking Lynn out for the first time, which was almost a year after LuAnn's death, he counseled with his children. They all said, "Sure, Dad, that's fine." But several weeks later when they found out he was dating Lynn, they sounded different. It became clear that Lynn was not the problem, but they felt LaMar was dating too soon. They were not ready to see their dad with someone other than their mother.

"My children all knew Lynn before I started dating her," LaMar said. "It just took some time for them to feel com-

fortable with the idea of me choosing to be so close to someone else. They all reminded me that she could never be
Mom. But within a year, they had obviously accepted her into the family and were feeling good about my being with her
and seeing me happy. My daughter refers to Lynn as her Second Mom."

LaMar struggled to know whether or not it was too soon
as he realized his strong feelings for Lynn. He talked to his
counselor again. The counselor pointed out that loving two
people at once, each in a different way, is what we all do all
the time. LaMar found it very helpful and freeing to con-
clude, "I can love several children at once, each in a different
way, and I can also love two women at once, since one is
gone and the other is present." He sees this counsel as part
of the Lord's leading.

Lynn and LaMar saw that neither of their houses suited
both of them together, so they found a house that did.

"We had no real problems about sharing things," LaMar
says. "Lynn is so appreciative of the things that were Lu-
Ann's; she is so accepting of my former life. We both enjoy
using the dishes that LuAnn and I received from her mother for our wedding, and the special dishes Lynn had from her
family. I think we are both proud of each other's families
and glad to share that part of the past. There's no reason to
be defensive or apologetic."

About money, LaMar says, "It's nice to share a combined
pocket. But we each have a 'hobby fund,' a sum we have in
mind, kept track of rather casually, that we can each use for
our own hobbies without feeling we are stepping out of
bounds."

From the first date, LaMar knew where he wanted to get
married. He says, "It was great Lynn felt the same way."
They had once gone to a candlelight program at a nearby his-
toric site. Due to his five years in Africa, LaMar had not

heard this kind of choral music for quite a while and was overwhelmed—not only with the music, but also with his fledgling emotions for Lynn. "The place did it to me," LaMar teases. "I thought, 'Oh, God, this place, this woman.' In the quietness of my own heart, I felt this woman by my side and I knew she would be a special friend."

Then on the way home, friends with whom they had spent the evening, commented that the place where they had just been would be a wonderful setting for a wedding. And somehow that evening LaMar knew that he wanted to marry Lynn, realizing that if her cancer did come back, he did not want to watch from a distance. He wanted to walk with her through it. (See more about their wedding at the museum in Chapter Four.) He says, "The wedding clearly marked a new beginning for both of us."

The most difficult part in the whole story for LaMar was just putting his past life to rest. But his greatest joy is realizing he can dream again. "I have similar dreams now as before," he says, "but I will live them out with another love. Knowing that LuAnn and Lynn knew and loved each other helps greatly. I just try to go carefully over the bittersweet parts. Lynn lets me be me, not probing, because she knows I have thoughts, at times, that I cannot easily share. That also brings joy."

"Whatever happens," LaMar concludes, "the Lord makes a way."

BEULAH'S STORY

Beulah and Harvey knew each other since they were children. Both of their spouses had died on the mission field. On his way to North America from Africa, Harvey sent Beulah, still in Africa, a card from a place he visited. Beulah had been determined never to remarry. Then she came across the verse in 2 Chronicles 30:8,

"Do not be stiff-necked, as your fathers were; submit to the Lord. . . . Serve the Lord your God, . . ."

Three things stood out to her—don't be stiff-necked, yield to the Lord, and serve the Lord. Beulah feels that this verse may have been the key to her being willing to consider marriage to Harvey. She realized he needed a wife. The mission board had told him he should not come back to Africa until he married again. They corresponded until she went to North America the next year. "I still had some questions," she says, "but in God's timing and with his leading, we married and went back to Africa together."

18.
A SECOND HUSBAND'S STORY

David became a second husband when he married Donna. At the same time, he became father to Donna's four children, ranging in age from two to nine years. Donna's husband had been killed in a traffic accident.

David says, "While ready to begin a companionship that would end in marriage, at age 27 I was as single as ever. God knew where I stood in regard to desiring a lifelong companion, but his answer seemed slow in coming. I had talked with my pastor, questioning whether I needed to get into more singles circles. My faith wasn't perfect, but for the most part I did leave the matchmaking process up to God."

It seemed to David like a divine appointment when he discovered that another young man had the same vision as he, to reach out to fatherless boys in their congregation. During the summer they spent a fair amount of their free time with this "great group of boys." It was as part of this ministry that David started picking up Donna's oldest son, Jon, for outings. He soon found that he needed to pick up Jon ahead of schedule so he had enough time to talk longer and longer with Jon's mother.

After a while, Donna called David to ask whether he was taking her son on outings because of his interest in her. He told her, no, that was not the reason. But he called her back a few days later to confess that he was interested in her, but that he had no hidden motives about relating to her son.

One of his biggest fears had to do with his ability to support the family, but when he expressed this concern to Donna, she assured him that there was other income available. That relieved him of that barrier, and he began to think of marrying her as a possibility.

"I must say," says David, "it was not without a myriad of questions, doubts, and long talks with good friends and family that our relationship began, but there was also a glimmer of hope."

He admits that the relationship was not all smooth and easy. They both had their share of doubts during their dating time and wondered how in the world it could work. It seemed that when Donna questioned the relationship, David felt good about it, and when he had doubts it was her turn to feel good.

David says, "I was more sure than she was; I was ready for this. We put off being engaged until the next spring. She needed this time to adjust to the idea of marriage."

Their wedding in November was a great celebration. His vows quoted here in part show that he was committed and happy about the step they were taking:

". . . Here are my goals and commitments and, with God's help, what I will strive to fulfill and accomplish until the day we separate by death.

"I promise to love you above all other people and things, second only to God himself. I commit myself to loving you not only when I feel like it and when it's easy but also on the days when I'd rather think only about myself. Loving you unconditionally means I will love you when you're having a bad day, feeling overwhelmed, having an attitude problem . . . If something changes your outward appearance I will still love you.

"I promise to consult with you before deciding to do anything that will affect you or the children. Regardless of what I feel God is calling us to, I commit to being in agreement with you before acting on that call.

"I also promise to love your children as my own, to share in parenting and the disciplining of these four precious gifts in an equal way.

"I promise to communicate with you about the hard things as well as the fun things, the everyday as well as the unusual. I promise to share with you my dreams and visions, my doubts and fears. I will communicate more in quantity and quality with you than with anybody else. I will be faithful to you alone, both mentally and physically.

"I promise to be your most intimate accountability partner. I commit to challenging you to become all that God wants you to be and not settling for less. I will encourage you to stay in the Word and in fellowship with the Father always, and I commit myself to doing the same.

"I promise to love you, to get to know you more and more, to cherish you, to build you up, and to never leave you until the day God calls me home. *I love you Donna!!*

Then David spoke these vows to the children:

"Jon, Doug, Cindy, and Scott, today I promise to be your new father. For the rest of my life I will be there for you. I wish I could say I'll be the perfect daddy for you, but I'll fail sometimes (like I already have at times), and I'll need you to forgive me and tell me when and how I hurt you.

"Maybe sometimes you'll wish you had your first daddy. And, that'll be okay, even though it will hurt. I'll try to talk about it with you whenever you want. Even though it will be hard sometimes, I'm looking forward to being your dad (if you don't mind), and I love each of you very much. And . . . that . . . will never ever change."

Donna told her own very personal story at the wedding. Here is part of it:

"I praise God for bringing me to this point where I am to-day. For God has truly walked with me through the difficult experience of Darryl's death and has helped me to begin again with a new relationship.

"I remember sometime after Darryl's death, when I was praying and asking God about a husband and whether he would have me marry again, he showed me the verse, 'No good thing does he withhold from those whose walk is blameless'(Psalm 84:11). I took that as meaning he would give me another husband and not withhold this from me.

"So I continued praying and asking God to show me if that really was God's will for me and, if so, to lead me to that person. I didn't want to just date around, and I decided to wait at least a year before starting a new relationship. There were different men who were interested, but, as I got to know them, I felt the best about David! We had gradually gotten to know each other, and it was a year later that we actually started dating. I was amazed as I discovered some of the similarities between David and Darryl. I saw in David a real love for God and his Word, a very disciplined life, a servant's heart, a real giver, good values, and a strong love for children. David even played guitar and wrote songs as Darryl also did. My love for David grew, and, when I began to feel his love for me and my children, and in turn their love for him, I began to feel that maybe God was drawing us together. I could see David fitting into the role of husband and father, and I began to see him as truly being a gift from God!

"But I had a hard time receiving that gift sometimes, because many questions and doubts would surface in my mind like, why would God give me someone so wonderful as David? He's too good for me. How can he love me? Can he love my children as his own? Why does he want all this responsibility of a family? What if it doesn't work out? What if I lose him, too? And on and on.

"As our relationship continued, I began to realize where some of my questions were coming from. Having been in a relationship for 11 years with Darryl and getting to that point of closeness, I expected it to happen immediately with David, but I realized the blending process needed to take place all over again.

"As we got to know each other and discovered our differences and how to work through them, we saw how we could complement each other. I needed to adjust to sharing my responsibilities with David, after learning to take care of myself. I needed to lay down my rights and my control of things.

"Also, doubts and fears surfaced at times when I struggled with a low self-image. I felt like I wasn't good enough for David. I also feared that if I shared my life and my love with David, it might somehow take away from the intimacy I had with God."

And then she turned to David and said to him, "But David, I want to thank you for being patient with me in those doubting times, for continually assuring me of your love and commitment to me and the children. As I reflect back on all the ways that you showed your love to me and the children, I have to wonder why I even questioned your love at all. Like the times you kept the children for me so I could run errands or spend time alone. And when I'd come home there'd be supper on the table and an extra casserole in the freezer for another meal. You taught me the benefits of making double batches when I cooked."

She continued addressing her wedding audience, "I loved the surprise notes I'd find all over the house—notes expressing his feelings of love for me, affirmation to me, and sometimes Scripture verses. I'd find them in my clothes closet, on the bathroom mirror, in my drawers, on the cupboards, in the freezer. I even found one in my flour canister that said, 'You are loved.'"

And to David, Donna continued:

"I remember you'd call me almost every day, sometimes just to tell me you love me and to hear how I'm doing. You'd play guitar and sing to me or read Scripture over the phone to encourage me.

"You spent many an evening helping me bathe the children and get them all ready for bed and read to them, talking and praying with them by their bedsides, even when it was late and you needed to go to work that night. And you'd do it all with a good attitude and without complaining.

"You always saw to it that there was a container of cleaned carrots in the frig 'cause you wanted to be sure the children ate right, and you're still trying to get them to eat salads!

"I remember the time when I was in a bad mood and you told me to spend the evening sleeping, and not to do the dishes or the wash, and that you'd take all the children to Jon's ball game and do the work when you got back.

"I loved seeing the children curled up around you on the sofa as you read to them, and I loved seeing them run out the door and down the sidewalk to greet you when you came, saying, 'David's here!'

"I love your sense of humor and how you made me laugh again and enjoy life more and feel 'young' again. I'll never forget the night I heard music outside my bedroom window, and, when I looked out, there you were, playing your guitar and singing a song to me that you wrote—your proposal song to me":

Can you hold me in your heart forever?
Will you patiently walk with me
And leave me never?
Can you say you'll hold me close
As a constant friend and lover?
Can you hold me in your heart, forever?

Dear Donna, won't you be mine?
I love you so;
It's hard to trust;
I see your fears,
But won't you let them go?
Most every day I pray for you;
I wanna see you be set free.

May you walk in Faith,
In trust, in love;
Believe in God and me.
You're the one I choose today;
Will you marry me?

I'm not naive—
Four little ones . . . It's true
Ain't gonna be a breeze.
But I think we've got just what it takes
To be a team and a family.
With lots to balance we'll need the Lord. . . . to
Keep our priorities.

Donna continued her story:

"You were the one who encouraged my children to use three words, 'Thank you' and 'Please,' and to behave better in church. I remember the time we sat down and wrote a list of rules and manners for the children to follow. As I observed your patience, gentleness, and affection toward the children, and the time you took to play with them, it helped me to be more that way. I remember the children asking, 'Is David coming out today?' or 'When is David going to be here?' They love you, David. And I love you very much.

"I remember one day God showed me clearly that you are a gift to me, not because I deserve it, but because God loves me, and that this gift is not meant to harm, so I don't need to be afraid. It's meant to bless me and help me. My only obligation is to take care of it, cherish it, and treat it with love, and that's what I want to do! So I thank God today for all he has done for me and for his faithfulness to me."

This is the song David wrote, played on his guitar, and sang for the children at the wedding:

Today we become a family;
Jesus answered my prayer;
He gave me your wonderful mother
And put each of you in my care.
I feel like you're my very own;
I love you with all my heart.
I thank the Lord for each of you
And pray we never grow apart.

And I'm sorry you lost your daddy;
He took good care of you.
He was a loving father
And a man of God through and through.
I'll never be able to take his place;

I'll be a different dad–brand-new.
So have patience with me,
And I'll do my best;
I'm your Daddy Number Two.

Now Jon, you're the oldest, obedient and talented.
Doug, you've got the patience;
You're a farmer and a fisherman.
Cindy, my little sweetheart,
so questioning and innocent.
Scott, you're the fast growing baby;
You're so cheerful and you're my little shadow.

Oh you're all so special, so special to me,
I'm so thankful God made us a FAM-I-LY.

After the wedding, David moved into the house where
Donna and the children had lived with Darryl. David adopt-
ed the children so they would all have the same last name.

David is patient with Donna as she deals with some ongoing fears. She says, "My biggest fear was losing David. I
was insecure and jealous when he'd talk to another woman.
There was no reason for it, but I still had the feeling."

Donna saw a counselor, and, through time, she experienced healing and has become more confident. But if she
hears a siren, she still thinks, "Where is David? Where are
the children?"

When seven-year-old daughter, Cindy, came with her
school class to see the farm, David noticed that she stayed behind in the milk parlor looking around. He thought it may
have been part of her way of grieving. She was about three
when her daddy died. David wrote this song and sang it for
her:

Jesus sees your tears; he feels the pain you feel,
He understands the sadness your little heart must bear.

He understands your questions, your doubts and
    your fears,
So give them all to Jesus, He'll take your every care.

At times you wonder how it might have been,
Your daddy as a farmer, working on the farm.
How would he laugh and smile, and talk and really be;
What would it be like with just, Mommy, Daddy, and me?

He was taken quickly, so little time;
You hardly got to know him, just doesn't seem fair.
Oh God, why my daddy? Why did it have to be mine?
Why must I bear this heartache? Please heal this heart
    of mine.

My dear little Cindy, the answers are few;
The questions are many, but of this I am sure:
That Jesus loves you deeply, he'll never leave you alone;
He'll be forever faithful, till he leads you home.

David relates some unusual experiences Donna had because of the fact that her first husband died on duty as a fire-
man. She was invited to a memorial service for fallen fire-
fighters and policemen. The committee had invited the President of the United States, but he could not be there, so, as a
token of his support, he invited the committee to choose one
family to meet with him in the White House. Donna and the
children were chosen, and they went, along with Darryl's parents. Donna gave the president a tape of Darryl's song and encouraged him to seek the Lord as he leads the nation.

His reaction was, "Thank you, and that's what we try to
do here."

The Lord was also honored through the newspaper arti-
cles covering Darryl's death. The family got to meet the Gov-
ernor of Pennsylvania; in addition the children have been
promised a free state university education.

Donna and David concur that God is too wise to make mistakes, too good to be unkind, and they go on trusting him.

JANETTE'S STORY

Janette's first husband died suddenly in a truck accident when she was only 29. Lonely and wishing to marry again, she prayed, telling God what she wanted—a man who was not married before, or at least had no children. But finally she prayed, "Okay, God, if he has children and needs a wife, I am willing." Soon thereafter, a man knocked at her door and asked directions to a neighbor. She gave him directions and he left. When he called her several days later, she learned that he hadn't really needed directions, but had stopped in order to see her.

She says, "I wasn't interested at first. He was 20 years older than I, he had a big business, and he had children."

He called again and asked, "Why don't we go out to dinner together?" She agreed and went, but she didn't agree to another date. He called again and asked if she needed someone to shovel snow. Her lane had already been opened, but they talked and then made plans to get together again.

"It was different from what I had asked God for," Janette says, "but in this marriage my childhood dreams were realized—and we could travel! I had hard times, too, but God has blessed me."

ABOUT THE AUTHOR

Martha Denlinger Stahl is a native of Lancaster County, Pennsylvania. She was an elementary school teacher for 20 years. Her M.Ed is from Millersville (PA) University.

This is Martha's third book. Currently she lives in a retirement community, where she continues to write, lead singing, and volunteer. In addition to teaching Sunday school, she also enjoys reading, needlecraft, traveling, bird-watching, watercolor-painting, word puzzles, and playing Scrabble.